The
Land Erotic

THE LAND EROTIC

A Memoir of Acres, Ecstasy &
Marriage in Midlife & Beyond

SUE WESTWIND

SAY YES QUICKLY BOOKS

Also by Sue Westwind:
Lunacy Lost: A Memoir of Green Mental Health

Say Yes Quickly Books
7715 East Highland Avenue
Scottsdale, Arizona 85251 USA
https://sayyesquickly.net

Front cover photograph: lolostock / Alamy Stock Photo
Interior typeface: Crimson

The Land Erotic / Sue Westwind. -- 1st ed.

ISBN: 978-0-9965592-8-7

For K., of the sideways smile at a good story

For ecstasy is not a simple or even pleasant experience ...
it transforms all previous assumptions and understanding.

—RACHEL POLLACK

NOTE:
*All events described in this book are true to the author's eye
and ear. Family members' names are pseudonyms.*

BOOK ONE

1

The day before we married, Asa and I took possession of the land. April Fool's Day: we would forever reference his "What Have We Done?" speech, made as we surveyed our new living quarters and swallowed hard.

A back door gaped onto the driveway. A urine-stained porch smelled of canines past. Inside, holes in the walls begged for new sheetrock and the floors for decorum. We didn't just buy a house, my idea of a charming project. The land, a lolling presence wet with spring rain, breathed life into our expectations. Asa's hopes seemed aligned with mine.

The realtor took us on a difficult hike around the perimeter, which paid off for him as our enchantment grew. Following barbed wire that encapsulated the sale, I peered into the woods' green light. What I didn't say to Asa and the silent moneyman was that I had waited all my life for this.

What stokes the hunger in a woman for land? Don't women want houses they can decorate with small mementoes and warm fabrics, not acres so dense with trees you can't fathom the end? Women who want rooms with forced air streaming from vents may note the lovely backdrop of thickets from their windows, but how many lust to go into the near-impenetrable as far as they can, reluctant to return? If I hadn't become betrothed to a piece of land soon, something was bound to boil over within me.

The year was 1993. I liked everything about how those numbers hung together, the factored and final emphasis on three. How three moves beyond the easy comfort of either/or, this/that. Action, reaction, synthesis. Triangles delight with their sturdy base and aspiring point. Triads and holy trinities dot mythologies of the world. And of course: mommy, daddy, and baby make three.

But the need for land stretched way back to wonder coupled with loss, in a way no one prepared me for: a child watching her grandparents' farm recede from the rear window of the family car heading back to the suburbs, while she strained to comprehend why we had to leave. Even in predictable yards all in a row, I experienced an unexamined gratification from sitting on ground that met me with clover or sand, red dirt or limestone slab as kids sprawled with play suspended—and the letdown when parents yelled us indoors.

I believed that someday we—my place and I—would meet daily for conversation, affection, and mystery. By midlife I was worn down by faces, sidewalks, stores, big plans, and the ever-tempting lure of the next new thing. I was disenchanted with my work as a therapist. The flit in and flit out of suffering humans in my office, once so rewarding, left me with a disconcerting sigh when I reviewed my calendar for the week. Compassion fatigue: it was time to turn inward.

There was more. I wanted to give birth and raise a child and could not imagine going it alone. I viewed those women who chose that solitariness, or were thrust there, as warriors far out of my league. Besides, I was pushing forty. The edict "better late than never" blared in my head. I knew there were risks, but bravado wrestled with naivete for the willingness to jump in.

Beyond its beauty, there were practical reasons for us to buy the place—a nod toward investment, a bit of fiefdom on which to household, the potential of supplemental income—all good cover for an incurable yen. But though I was out of patience with living in town, the endeavor marked more than a vague *time to settle down*. It cemented our togetherness, this new groom's and mine, a bold start after both of us had left ruins behind.

The day we met the land, Asa walked his country walk, wearing cowboy boots that weren't allowed at the office. He was born into the routine of seasonal fields and stomped pastures; he knew how to herd cows and drive a combine. But he left that life as soon as he could, for college at age sixteen. He'd been marked as different from the start anyway with the strange name his mom so liked because it meant "born in the morning" in Japanese—and so he was, born on a morning in Japan.

The small farming community thought *Asa* was Hebrew, equally strange, for not a Jew lived in the county. His mother asked if he wanted to change his name, but he bucked at the thought, for it was *his* name. He told her a proud, "No." Besides, the name carried an echo of their shared trauma in Japan. There he was, Asa of complex beginnings adopted by a thoroughly WASP enclave, accepted but always a visible reminder of the way his mom returned in disgrace from her sojourn with his birth father, something never discussed. On the day we met the land erotic, as I would come to call it, Asa's family fields still thrived, but my grandparents farm was long deceased, sold for car dealerships and motels.

During that first trek around the perimeter of what was calling to become ours, Asa and I didn't talk, let alone share farm memories. The realtor, resigned to getting his shoes dirty, grew up on a working spread nearby, no stranger to muddy Herefords or plots of field corn, although he aspired to sell lavish condos in the distant metropolis. None of us could afford the vulnerability to peek from beneath our veneers of adults pretending to view a thing inert.

Silently, I claimed the place for Asa and me.

Finally! No more the city cousin visiting acres upon acres where every inch was in use, pancaked by cattle poop and sentineled by silage towers. My only job as a kid had been to jump on a horse and get out of the way, to work the reins past corrals and milkhouse. But this place where I walked through brush over craggy ledges with Asa? I could already hear it whispering *take me, make me.*

Most of it was densely wooded, some would say neglected. Ten cleared acres at the center elevation hadn't seen dryland farming in years. It looked nothing like the fields of Asa's youth, and I knew he suppressed the visceral rebuke—*please not even the thought of farming, hell no.* Later he did admit to a lust for a tractor of moderate size, a weekend toy. We weren't to the back border before I could read his approval of the place, sense him settling into the idea of attachment.

The money, signing of papers, and move were arduous enough as we combined two households, and my world burgeoned in size. "Land baroness!" Asa teased. Sixty acres were a bucket-drop compared to the holdings we knew as kids, but within these woods we prepared to cocoon.

Bone-tiring hours and an intimacy with lumber and hardware stores sustained our labors nightly. I loved the physicality of demolition, smacking down walls and ripping out nails. As newlyweds, it was sumptuous to feel the surrounding quiet of our bedroom without strangers on the other side of townhouse walls—come as loud as you please. The land also screams with a headlong blitz to promulgate.

Meanwhile, a rushing creek called beyond stacks of drywall and paint cans. "Property" wasn't something to bolster the ego when rattled by comparisons to others' possessions, or for that matter when looking into the void. Not this place, anyway. It was a relationship from the get-go. I thought I knew what I sought when it came to living in the country, but I had it all wrong.

Despite the pomp of surveys and appraisals, I never really believed the land was a chunk of dirt; a place owns itself. Asa agreed in theory but looked mystified when I suggested the land might double as a school. A mystery schools. I wanted to obtain knowledge of an art that had no name, a curriculum that formed itself day by exploratory day. Asa simply stared: his wife was weird. Back then weird was sexy, challenging, and only "dangerous-maybe."

The woods and the husband melded as inseparable gifts. I assumed my beloved had matching hungers for our new place, but there lies a newlywed flaw: *I know you feel just like I do!* I was eager to be done with cleanup and remodel, ready to expand to the outdoors. Whatever we did there, it would surely be rife with lessons. At last, we moved our sights past the house. But it was clear my new husband didn't come outdoors for an education.

He came to work for sore muscles, grappling with hand and power tools, re-creating highly selective enactments of the full-scale farm he grew up on. Chickens topped his agenda, along with vegetable gardening. He constructed the hens' shed, he rototilled, and he heaved post-hole diggers into the soil to mark the garden plot—sown in the straight-row pattern he knew from every wheat and sorghum seed drilled into his childhood.

Enamored, I was the pupil who took part one step removed, for Asa was raised on a real farm. I tagged along, attentive, toting tools, clearing debris, plunking seeds in straight rows when my visions were of seedlings congregating in circles, bulging over raised beds, messy but opulent gangsters showing their colors and height.

Asa sidestepped his painful past of country living. He kept to a weekend homesteader's fantasy—the small scale, do-it-yourself satisfaction he wanted to indulge. But I'd learn soon enough what called up the specter of Pops—his dad, the dedicated farmer, forever unavailable, out in the field. Pops used that identity in every feasible way to distance from his family and condemn them to hell for sloth and impiety.

By contrast, my Irish Catholic grandparents gave me a playground to grow up in that saved me from uniform neighborhood grids when vacation was on my parents' minds. I hung out with cows, monstrosities who bawled and wore muck and shit without care. But mostly I rode my beloveds—quarter-horse, palomino, appaloosa—bereft when it was time to say goodbye to their regal flesh and attentive personalities.

"We will have horses here," I said to Asa.

Boy-owner of a Shetland pony, he spun around and replied, "Are you kidding? They smell bad! You can't get that stink off you."

What? The scent of horses is ambrosia!

If only our differences could have hovered permanently on such lightweight preferences.

I knew Asa's father was a thorn in his side, but just how badly I had yet to learn. Why did my new spouse jump into tasks as if the specter of Pops hovered with every switch-on of the circular saw? Because he was blending the Home Improvement craze with the easy knowledge of tools learned in Pops' toolshed, and initially the recall was sweet. It was seasoned by his grasp of a need for a hobby when the suit and tie came off. Besides, with his eye for detail he could likely out-finesse the Pops who had been an absence, obsessed with his far-flung fields, neglecting the family house, pissing off the landlord who threw them all out at last and burned the place to the ground. Pops never mentored Asa at man stuff or farm stuff; son went into the shed when father was away and learned on his own. He was curious then, about everything, marked early as the one to haul up roots and migrate out of reach.

When I watched him in the shop after dark, moving under brash hanging lights, it anchored me. His obsession with tools was so far out of my grasp it was a novelty, as though they were toys but then again, such baffling utility. I looked up to Asa when he was in the tool zone, manipulating their heft and length for his makings. It wasn't like me to find such blatantly masculine pursuits a thrill.

I was an intellect-freak, a "sensitive man" junkie. Asa had the smarts and sensitivity, blended in a way that fit no mold. In the middle of tree-cloister and creek habitat, we were free to shrug off the scrutiny of our midlife marriage by old friends and acquaintances.

Tentative about many things of the world, I tended to race full speed into them initially, then crash into paralysis about the next move. I was the one who found the land, who finagled the down payment, who pulled most of the strings to get the wedding to come off without a hitch. I did it for him, for me, for us, but now? How was I to keep impressing him? I didn't want more commotion. I wanted to be married and live countrified. Let the days rub like satin with peace and delight handed over by the awareness of here and now.

But once the house was livable, there emerged a shift in Asa's focus. He stopped wanting to seek out the woods, let alone skirt the boundaries of our land. He commandeered the garage and chicken shed, changed the oil in the cars, and wielded a chainsaw into shoulder-aches that lasted for days. Then came the sullen mood, the letdown over never getting enough done. "Relax," I cajoled, "who's task-mastering you? Nobody, not even them chickens!"

While I churned with excitement about our new life, Asa took to the outdoors with grim determination and gruff complaint. Such had been the way of the man who once farmed and fed him, not given to show delight or appreciation for nature. Nature was livelihood, do or die, and Asa fell into this stoic, slightly put-out role in a matter of weeks. He ventured outside and forgot the reality of the gentleman-farmer he was. He spent most of his hours commuting to manage a gaggle of young interns and solve the problems of demanding clients. It was as if, when he threw off the sport coat to don the Carhartt jacket, he donned a faulty accessory: the stoop-shoulders of stepdad, the danger-man.

Pops toiled in soybeans and sunflowers four-hundred miles away and never visited, but I could see in my husband's eyes and hear it in his voice: somehow the man invaded our land. I should have called an exorcist—in modern times, a therapist. One can't be one's husband's therapist. Asa insisted he'd never confront the stepfather who lived across the state anyway. Why should he? Whenever we made the long drive to the farm, we marveled at the old geezer's rewrite of history wherein Asa was the greatest of all sons ever. In private Asa declined to worry over the discrepancies between past and current versions of the story with the only mantra he ever applied to the situation: "What good would it do?"

But our land had no working fields, only woods and spots of prairie. I saw what I wanted to see: the land erotic in soft-bump hills, the peeping eyes of wild berries on gangly canes, the trees gathered in stately congress, the creek bank where fantasies would flourish. I was the one who slipped away after chores, when at last Asa was TV-tied and nursing bursitis with the umpteenth groan about how *that* was more work than he expected. It was easy to push off with the dog, both of us shadowed by companionable cats that lived in the barn. My husband found this escort fitting. He'd taken to the high plains with such feline fans in tow. With a nod we were off to our respective escapes.

Former owners left indelible marks on my green lover, and it pained me. Old tires, lone passenger seats, and miscellaneous axles dotted creek and pasture. Piles of trash, so deep into the soil, layers of trash over soil over trash that we finally stopped excavating and threw on a final dressing of cosmetic dirt. Before we arrived, the owners had pushed a makeshift cabin over the high edge of a ravine, creating a jumbled pile of weathered boards and beer cans. I could understand their statement: *do not plunder our memories.*

Still, I seethed at the sight of these things. I knew I could treat my land better. I wanted no reminders of anyone, except the ghostly Indigenous people's presence I was eager to learn more about. Their arrowheads and pottery shards were confiscated by the former trash-strewers though, a loss I mourned as when lovers who meet late in life imagine each other's youth. I ranged over, and into, the body of the land that was now mine, and felt the thrill that was part explorer, part despot.

What was it like to ramble during those first weeks? How I wish the metaphor would expand alongside a first kiss, first feel, the heat of foreplay. But the desire to draw close mixed with a certain will to conquer, the dark side of a love affair. I plotted the hacking of trails, the trimming of trees, and the renewal of pond into a natural bowl beneath a long channel of stones spilling downward. I pretended the land smiled on these dreams, for I was the new and improved helpmeet, a willing partner of this long-awaited dance where we would be sure to please each other.

I knew I needed Asa for my schemes. As my ever-practical spouse pointed out, we had so much to do with the house and yard before we could develop the land. My wishes for farther flung projects paled like urges for scenarios that simmer at the edges of desire, the kind your mate won't agree to enact.

No matter, it was easy to get pleasantly sidetracked alone. My vision clutched at circles of hawk and turkey buzzard, picturing how, with their wings and sharp vision, the trees gave way to tallgrass. Ten acres, flat and open with native fronds, crowned the central hill: "up top," we called it. I made my way, breathless with the effort, there for the sky.

Where the woods emptied me out onto an expanse, summers once saw the surge of rich alfalfa. Now native grasses made dense fluff for a suitable chaise lounge. I threw down a blanket and leaned back, snug among the stillness, drifting like a mote of gratitude in the secret heart of the land, asking to be shown how we were one and the same.

Back at the house, Asa would eventually rouse himself to pay bills, make phone calls, or look at client files, soaking up the bliss of belonging that his profession bestowed. My simple question was never answered: "If you love being a lawyer so much, why stress non-stop?" I felt guilty to revel alone in such unequaled joy: this was no one's land but "mine," Asa was "mine," this was life at last! *It's all right,* I thought, *opposites attract. So what if I like to sit and savor in a solitary way? He'll come around.*

The deer picked paths through the shade, the creek caressed rocks I'd not met, and an infinitude of pale roots twined beneath all that moved. To the land hypnotic, I pledged loyalty for life.

Wood Man

There's a man crossing my creek, heading for a hill that bares one shoulder into all I can see. He pauses and turns to stroll the edge of shallow water instead. Heading upstream, he winds his way, faithful to every bend—and I receive the idea that I'm to follow. I will trail behind his shirtless grace because I know every inch of this place, ravine by meadow by rocky slope, and I wonder: does he?

The creek slips through land tied to two names, my husband's, and mine. Our trespasser doesn't wear a speck of guilt. He picks up speed along the far bank where the woods thicken at his elbow. I need to catch up.

A rubble of limestone supports my quest across the creek. These hard heads groomed by sporadic rain are always there for me. They laugh at my desire to see the animal swish of the man's walk while they sit busy at silent prayer: every day the holy, every human an apparition to bear. The man treading here like he owns the place is probably known by the rocks as a harmless beast, an ally, maybe even kin. Their approval would recommend him highly.

With a glance in my direction—neither coy nor commanding—the man throws a thought that he learned these hills long before I came along. Which is why I keep going, closing the distance. His eyes match the winter-shade of an oak, gray turning silver when the sun is cold light. But his eyes are for later because I'm obsessed with his stride, undulating in the strangest pair of, I guess, pants.

His skin wears the tint of clay from surrounding soil, but that's fur below the waist. Yet those cheeks look human enough, and he leaves no sign of hooves—damp ground displays the oblongs of two soft feet. Gaining on him, this must be the appointed place. When he turns to face me, I see.

The whole concept of attire is eclipsed by the center of his body where the penis stands, ascending from small and tight curls. Way past reason or doubt I know that it is matched to the inside of me, tailored in size and shape to how this woman expands and contracts when the juices are flowing. This is how the land reaches in to one who comes to be its lover. How could I have expected less?

This man spirit, land spirit, is much more than fantasy-fodder. He obliges the vulva's appetite whenever I run outside to escape the din and dither of my house, the marriage that's stalled and can't find its way back to how it began. If I were another woman on a separate piece of ground the man might be bigger, or smaller, his organ might list to the left or to the right. He might skirt the creek in blue denim with porcelain features and not as a relative to some satyr on the run.

But he is willing to appear to every woman calling on Eros through her own beloved piece of Earth. He is the night voice at the edge of the yard, the herald of a morning freshly pulled from sun, the green stroke of underbrush along creek-edge and hills.

Women who take their place on the land, embedded and embodied, walk looking for him, memorizing every detail of his saunter and moods, each one wondering what happens if he turns out to be "real," wondering how he might fit inside the moon cave of her body and mind.

Especially a woman who sniffs tree bark savaged by a deer in rut and gravitates to the smell, aroused and uneasy about a force too brusque to explore with fingers or tongue. A woman excited when sunset throws a rough umber on prairie grass that swathes, for short moments, her entire world. A woman who whispers sweet nothings to a summer moon, its light a relic of humanity's less restrictive past. This is a woman who surrenders to the land erotic when it embraces her, held close in delectable silence.

I am she, and these are my thirsts on sixty acres I "own" with a husband. The satyr-man bounds away with a leap that is animal and impersonal, and I can only grind my hips against a fallen tree trunk for release of what has been building with every twist of his torso and limbs, every second of his shy exposure. When I shout, "My God!" it is to this entire place mating with itself, surging rhizomes below and hosting possum toes within the inane boundaries drawn by fence line and doing so whether I take another breath or not.

This is the land erotic, my most sacred conjugal visit, a private pastime when stumped for comfort among the stressed and striving that tear through their days indifferent to the pleasures of wild space. It is an academy, a monastery, and an everyday bacchanal—the most ancient of all meditations, a respite that encloses home.

≈

Woods, man. Wood Man. He is here, a traveler and a stay-at-home saint. Never the trespasser, he was here first and will stand to the last. My woods, any woods—most people don't look for him. It's the attire, and the constant erection that may be a disturbing delusion in your mind—that flesh-arrow pointing onward.

The old Wuduweard (Woodwards, guardians of the forest) grew their hair long and tried to emulate him, smelling of bark and struck humble before rings and rays revealed to the fresh cut. An uneasy truce between Wood and ordinary men continues: *I hear your song but need more frames and mantles and paper towels, and you will help me make them.*

But on the land erotic, trees yield to Wood Man as he frequents this land: they part and sigh, they die when lightning boils their cells alive, they brim with nuts that mimic a testicular rage for life. I prefer to name Wood Man their guardian, but he may be the woods' doppelganger walking. Once I thought I saw him taller than the clouds, with tree trunks for legs that were sensitive to my touch. He takes shape and texture to enthralling heights.

I have never loved like this—I'm speaking of the husband now. Wood Man knows all about it. He freely lets me exploit the seesaw between domestic *bliss*-krieg and my loose behavior in the wild. I feel no shame when I catch sight or scent of his steps, but there's no chance I'll tell Asa any of it.

Asa, framed by the house, Asa the indoor man, jobholder, bedmate. Asa, who is pale, bulky, and tender where the Wood Man is coarse and swathed in the pelage of introvert mammals. Wood Man understands how smitten I am by the indoor man, how I worry that I fabricated a satyr to extend Asa because Asa lacks the daring to see the Wood Man on our land. Am I a cheat?

Give me a half-hour in the trees and I can augment the soul of the marital relationship, find another way to get drunk on my passion for the flesh-man by releasing it into actual terrain. Or is it the other way around? I want something more than the walls where wildlife prints freeze movement into salutes to Nature, mostly waterfowl flying against clouds in a mood.

But here's the deeper question: is wandering the land in a tumult of imagination really the felt lash of a love-addict's desire, or the seep of spirituality under my skin? Wood Man could care less that I see him human-esque. But how do I ably picture any true force driving the seasons under sun and stars?

Wood Man knows I hunt him. For a glimpse, for a jolt to the nostrils that derails speech, for a psalm's cry to inspire the marriage destined for midlife and beyond. The hunt may be sprinkled with sexual fantasy, but it is advanced by adulation of the most fearless kind. So let us pray—just in case it is a god I'm asking for in every orgasm, here in the lumpy-ground shade or between the conjugal sheets:

Wood Man, eternal soul of recurrent forests that pucker the prairie with hickory and oak, I lay my grateful mess upon you. I am living the dream I could not live without. You called. I came. I looked for you elsewhere but now we are together. You are no more capable of leaving me than my own hand detaching itself from my infatuation.

Wood Man, you glimmer in the beloved who shares the house, but you are the whole House, the backdrop that holds "a new couple" in suspension as we lunge for happiness as friable as ash in the wind.

Here among the private acres of my utter exaltation, let new life burgeon from heresy: I will no longer be a beacon for others' tales of suffering.

I quit my job, the dress code, and the schedule—for now. I planned to wade close to what's usually overlooked, leave the known paths inside this fenced but riotous space, until I walk back out a Wood Woman fully done with cynical youth's horrendous waiting game.

2

The scrawniest tree stood apart, and what a deer did to it wasn't pretty. There are trees and more trees on my land, but I don't like to see one wounded. I confess that's not what drew me to this one though.

It was the smell.

The tree and I were the same height, and I thought about how to address it. What a revelation when I learned to tell hardwoods from each other by name, how to speak the signatures of evergreens that bore a deep emerald shade throughout the cold. It was like gaining a community where everyone revealed exactly who they were. Songs of nomenclature were simple pleasures to chant while gazing on those standing: *Chinquapin, Hackberry, Juniper, Elm!*

But without leaves I can't always identify the genus, and this poor thing had given up its green flags. Skinny-bare, gouged bark, and only a reek of distinction came from the scrape.

It was maleness, animal pure.

A randy buck went after the young tree with an antler, to signal the available females in the area. We like to think he's nicking the velvet off his rack because his headgear itches, but that's seldom so. Mature bucks will chafe and smear to leave a message, a number where they can be reached.

Why do we call the state that addles them a *rut*?

Because it feels like one? Lust without satiety can get monotonous, though one might wish for such a delightful holding pattern. I stood next to the scruffy tree and felt a shift.

Was it wrong or was it weird—that I could be aroused by a male from another species like that, his scent left behind on the tree? It's not as though I wanted to be present if the big guy charged back into the area. The moment didn't so much grab my crotch as massage some other membranes accordingly. The land erotic, up your nose.

Was the scent from the damaged tree a link to my fantasy man scouting the woods, enticing me into a scavenger hunt for joy? Could he, in some way of looking at the world, be real?

Shamans tell how they sync their minds into animal bodies. Often, it's a soaring beast of prey—birds lend themselves to merger, I think, because one of the soul's wildest longings is to fly. In REM sleep, dreams of flight can culminate in orgasm. I understand how perching on the strong shoulders of a dreamtime eagle could trip a switch—the wide back and unequaled loft, the natural majesty of that much strength.

But the man I was beginning to see in the woods—the satyr with his smudged face—is firmly grounded and most of the time hidden. His is a shifting palette of odors, the clever broadcasting of desire. Who wants to become animal enough to experience something that unsettling? I worried about whether this battered tree's wound would close. At the same time, I longed to possess and become possessed by a man half-beast in these woods. While hunting for him I couldn't be held accountable for trampling or tearing a few green things in my haste.

If there are lessons in how to experience the rut as deer do, I'm inhaling deep—because something in me is identical to that urge, a buck rubbing his HERE I HORNY AM all over the woods for miles until one doe, nostrils flaring, twitches her tail in heat.

Sunset can be a sensual rush if you let it.

Sometimes I need to flee my land for another perspective. Often there is the lust for water, big water, or as big as it gets around here.

Forty years and no one thinks about how a reservoir filled. The lake is a fringed bowl claiming all eyes. Only the massive stretch of dam shouts *manufactured*. When I climb the overlook, I can't help but think of the towns erased when the Army Corps of Engineers began to dig. Generations of memories layer under the water.

I'm smitten by the reach of it, thirty-five square miles, lying like a lounger with no distractions save the occasional dot of motorboat or flicker of sail. It takes five minutes to scurry down and see what's lapping at the edge.

Height is different on this jewel of a lake as opposed to my land's more subtle elevations. At home I climb and know I'm climbing up top—then everything is horizontal again. On the mound at lake's edge, I am a lookout, surrounded by air, facing water on three sides with a slope that took my breath behind me. There is no other reason to be here than to feast the eyes. At most, a dozen persons could congregate on this tip. What might we come to see? How the sun goes down away from town.

I can't stay here; I must descend to see the sky bleed, so I slip partway on my ass, scuttle perilously at an angle the rest of the way in loose dirt that resembles a path but is only jesting—it's a slide. At last, my spot for the show. I love the dusk, love the transition. But even better is what I call The Pinking.

One freak warm winter evening, the mound and the shore are thick with couples in shirt sleeves. I'm the practical one toting jacket and gloves—as the sun fades, I'll be toasty and vindicated. How did all these young people know it was going to be an erotic sunset tonight? Call it the lovers' hunch.

There is no pink like this sky. *Hot* pink? This sky is a five-alarm fire. And tonight, I know why everyone is standing still, transfixed. The swath made by the sun's leaving is huge and hangs down into the water. Despite a silver cuff at the shore, the whole lake burns as the sky slips in extra sheen and churns fuchsia on the waves. There is too much vibrancy here for the air to handle. When the sky stoked itself into a hue beyond compare, it simply had to share.

I run back up the mound because I want to see every wisp of it and suddenly, I want it from a height, aware that I'm turning my back on milliseconds I could be imbibing, then embarrassing myself when I see two persons seated on the path ahead—she enclosed in his arms, as intent on the pinking as me. I'm an older woman scuffling up the trail and stopping to look back, my body language urgent. But I won't reach the summit in time. Instead, they get to drink it all in—will it help or hinder them tonight? Do they know how lucky they are? They stir and make to leave as I approach a little more nonchalantly, swerving into the weeds to accommodate their murmuring.

I exult because the pinking is wanton; it spreads, so vivid it dwarfs anything moving on water or land. After a grand climax, it too fades. Geese float in procession before its denouement, the peacefulness of post-coital fervor claims the lake, and the whole scene is cinched when Venus, the evening star, winks on.

Now she is the show, the story-maker, shining with variegated blips and blinks onto dusky blue.

Should I be sorry for slinking here when I love my land so much, sorry for going wild for the pinking, for wishing upon Venus's golden point, wishing like it was my final wish from the genie?

And what is Asa doing right now?

Suddenly I'm too far from home.

An estranged friend got cancer and set out to make peace with everyone he'd ever loved and lost. I was on the list and touched by this effort one hears about in the dying. He beat the cancer—simply saying that doesn't do justice to what anyone goes through, the pain and fear and mess of it. He wished to see us.

Back in the day, the friend and Asa were in a men's group. One evening, I heard tell, my friend waxed ecstatically about his love for the natural world. In fact, he confided being so overcome by lust for Mother Nature that he found an indentation in her body and humped until his semen ran speckled with dirt. Yeah, I could see him doing that!

New Girlfriend sat bemused over spicy Indian food: "Did you *really* fuck a hole in the ground?"

He bristled at the coarseness of the word because what he was doing, he said with some pomp and snippiness, was *making love to the earth.* Her reply?

"No more ayahuasca for you!"

Asa and I waited to see if the inside joke would break open. What the hell was *aya*-what?

"Ayahuasca," my friend explained, "is all about the Earth."

He told us how tribes in the Amazon have long harvested the vine and its helper-plants, cooked them down to a vomit-inducing yet remarkably healing brew. In time white folk caught on, and lately they travel to the jungle to share in the mysteries, claiming cures of everything from cancer to dark depression. Priests of the vine guide novices past the puking and diarrhea to their personal heaven or hell. Outcome depends on how many hateful demons you harbor, and how well they hide in your mind from the awful-tasting truth serum.

I wish I had the courage to take that ride. It wasn't the first time I wavered about whether I needed a guru or a tradition or at least a practice that was more precise than wandering in trees and tallgrass as my inner bell called me.

Then I'd come home, be dropped to the ground by unplanned beauty and treated to a searing truth because I showed up on the land that day, shaken with a veracity I could no longer find in the eye of a human. My own mystery school, the land holding our house in its cupped palm, taught me not to shatter my brain and gut biome in order to dismantle my pain.

≈

Who's promoting fornication with trees like a fetish not yet sampled, a sexual consumer's new thrill? Not me. But would it bother a tree if we humans rubbed lasciviously against it? Bucks in rut do a lot more damage. How else to serve the love-seeking human heart, recall its body homeward, or expand the way we think?

I want to say that any erotic touch between the land and our hominid hulks is healing, and conducive to a trend to treat a place lovingly, be it tundra or tropics, glacier, or cedar-lined ravine. The land accepts and wishes to fondle the most private side of our flesh, the most vulnerable tips of glands and tunnels we crave to divest of shame. Do you turn from this idea in disgust? Then you may be exalting nature as mother-only at the expense of your animal soul.

Maybe if we envisioned a sunset pink as the center of sex spread onto the sky, we'd think twice about letting anyone release ground-level ozone into the troposphere. Mingling your cum into the forest floor, you might never let ancient roots be ripped out for yet another mall. If the rain and seas purposefully console and caress you, you're bound to react publicly to the microplastic miasma that threatens them. Such love is motivation to untangle these wrongs. Yet, misguided and prim, there is environmentalist indignation over such an idea as the land erotic.

I didn't come to my land aware of a sensual urge about the great outdoors. Was it an overactive imagination, a spill-over from the newlywed atmosphere, a cool idea I forced on myself? I couldn't align to any root cause. And why spoil it with a narrative that pigeonholes the experience into deviance? It was too delicious, and certainly did no harm. It was the hidden bonus, the course they don't mention when they say, "mystery school." I doubt I was the first to find a way into this secret curriculum.

Human touch is a vital necessity, but why limit us to each other? Without the wider potential of sensation that the natural world specializes in, human erotic touch becomes addictive, so laden with unrealistic expectations that one eventually rolls over to the other side of the bed, gasping for *space*.

It doesn't matter how you unveil yourself to the land, though. You might need boots to protect your feet or a hat to bargain with the sun—accommodations acceptable, but don't overdo it. Don a light robe and walk where you will not be disturbed. Go to a haven that exchanges your sullied breath for precious oxygen, receives your footfalls mindfully, and sees you as you really are—wild and mostly free.

Such pilgrimage, made daily or when the hard world presses you to fear, has potential to defrock that finger-wagging critic in the belfry of the mind that flogs you to get back to work, wash the car, buy and save, but most of all, *scour the longing for wildness from your heart before you do something rash!*

3

I finally accepted that Asa and I had real differences in the way we viewed the outdoors when I shared a wish to make love at one of the land's most beguiling spots. To conceive a baby—before we got any older—was the plan. A first for both of us. I wanted to slither on him in a niche of soft soil that overlooked the creek bend, at the very spot the furred wanderer crossed, and I'd followed. There was just enough room for a blanket where young trunks of redbud leaned in to create a canopy bed. I didn't know if I'd get pregnant there, but it was one of my first inklings about how to have a deeper connection with these acres of ours.

"Ticks!" Asa recoiled at the plan, putting away a ratchet wrench in the shop. "I hate ticks."

I looked at this farmer's son in his beige, outside-jacket, the simple coarseness of it separating our roles as when I accompanied him on building projects, carting levels, hammer, and screws, a little disoriented as blue collar and white collar flickered in jagged patterns over his persona. But of course, I let it go. A woman flush with honeymoon vigor hates to be pushed away, so I made it all about the crawly bloodsuckers and tried to see his point.

Passing the spot on my way to the creek, it never failed to impress. What a suitable trysting nook! One morning I noticed some stalks pushing up from the deadleaf floor. "Go ahead," I told them, "I won't be using this space."

They were tall and forceful, sharing no clue how they would unfurl, much less present a face to creek world. You'd think I'd never seen mayapples before because I didn't know what to call these queens. Unwind and commandeer they did, taking over the would-be lovers' bed.

Greeted by their parasols filling the alcove so apt for romance, I nodded, a spectator who understood. The mayapples waved in the spouse-spurned spot like a consolation prize, jungle hands with fingers splayed as if to reach out and grab each other. I loved them for showing up. That few feet of ground became a place where hot, steamy love was possible, if not consummated by the group of green beauties with their own bulges: fruit rumored to be lemon-like, exotic, and yellow as a black cat's eyes.

≈

I beseeched Asa to mow a circle in the woods I could have as my own. It was time to make a container, a classroom for serious earth-mysticism. I found a discernible spot by the creek, only ten strides from the mayapples, thirty feet round without felling a tree.

One sprawling Osage orange stood in the east. South and west held the stalwart energies of red oak. In the north was openness, where the hill to Up Top rose with its steep jumble of woody perennials. The circle was only a five-minute walk from the house but tucked in, with no glimpse of the residence possible

I brought rocks from the creek bed to mark the directions. Humans have forever hauled such purposeful loads for crafting a church in the open air. It was a simple act of disguised import, the stories of each stone locked within, and I'd never made anything like it.

I adopted certain correspondences to the cardinal directions and chose accordingly. A triangle of limestone dragged to stand before the sky and point upwards, facing dawn. In the south, curious red rocks left by glaciers—the red of passion, energy, fire. For water's agent in the west, I had my pick of interesting artwork where the creek fingered all manner of rock; I chose a sizable portfolio of solid waves, its scalloped edge like a hulking clam. North, symbol of the earth element, needed to be ordinary and pulled directly from the dirt, hence a fine pedestal of moss-coated rock laid supine. At the center, I placed thin limestone platters for an altar, with a vase to catch rainwater that got knocked over by wildlife passing through instead.

These rocks became oracles whose every line and swirl I studied, guidebooks for the direction they pinned. But most of what I did inside their embrace was attempt to figure out what to do.

I sat. I wrote. I took the sun naked. I was new to the land but comfortable with a body turned plumper in midlife. I rued the small airplanes that crisscrossed the sky—unable to calculate if they saw what they thought they saw—I felt peeped. If not for silence and escape from machinery, why was I here?

Asa's rejection of a sexual soiree in the mayapple bower was chalked up to my oddball nature—bit by bit, "weird" was becoming less appealing and more a conundrum for him. Not exactly squeamish about nature, the man had his peeves like anyone else. Mine are stinging insects—their kamikaze weapons make them a feared Other in my eyes, so hard to see the divine at work there. By contrast, the slow though determined tick is easily tweezered from mind and skin.

Ticks and sand—Asa hated both. The ocean was a faraway dream from the landlocked acres we settled our lives into. Sand he could avoid. But ticks? If you're going outside, apply the chemical repellant, or better yet, pungent essential oils, and hope for the best. Did Asa begin to avoid his shop and garden due to ticks?

In the beginning, I overlooked these things. "You're so OCD!" I joked. Much easier to tease with initials when we disagreed. Later it was obvious that my husband was often on edge about several things, charging from coast to coast as the primary breadwinner of our home, only at ease within the sexual moments cushioned by our wide king bed. And those moments would fade too soon.

OCD? The tag was thrown around like a joke in the culture at large, much like ADD, a moniker for wild children who can't sit still in school. I had a long history of chafing at diagnoses. I kept excusing the small though senseless urges that populated Asa's character, his insistence and explosive anger if thwarted.

Weren't they minor things? Insisting on weekend coffee from the designated "Sunday mug." Cute! Needing to set the car radio volume on an even, never odd, number. Funny! Raging if I didn't close the zippers on items for the laundry—no big deal! Obsessing far into the night over his work, the pressure obliterated by marijuana inhaled for blessed sleep. Understandable, given the range of his responsibilities.

The truth was that my career, a therapy practice I'd always conducted at my residence, was impractical in the country and I jumped at that rationale to pull the plug. Clients didn't want to drive twenty miles to see me, some of it on narrow gravel roads, even if I had a room in the new home with pale textured walls and more open space. I surely didn't want to rent an office in town and make the drive. Besides, I'd be pregnant any day now. Asa and I agreed on how my hiatus for the pregnancy and a bit more stay-at-home would unfurl. It was all planned out.

Why Not Mother Earth?

The Wood Man is of the land, but in those first months I also turned to the land as my mother, ready to welcome me to those ranks where birth bent time into holiness, or so I envisioned it in my late-bloomer midlife.

I'd seen her before.

Regarded during school hours in Catholicism's pew as Mary, standing on the silver crescent moon, she didn't have much to say. On cherished hikes and escapes from daily grinds, I relaxed into her secular name: Nature. But when feminism stormed the gates of religion, I clamored with the best of them for a god who looked like me, Goddess She. Among wild women circling in private festivals, I discovered her in face after face.

Indoors I set a shelf on two cinderblocks to designate an altar, a place where daydreams or insights could roost. I used the extra room and dotted it with tabletop statues: maiden warriors, big bellied bountifuls ready to birth, a robed crone pointing out the mysteries of death. I stared at them all as if they could speak. If only these were available when I was a girl settling for less because less was all there was, served up as if less was superlative, an exhortation embellished by housewives and nuns, nurses, and schoolteachers: "Be careful outside! You might get dirty."

But woman is Nature, if you consider the past—both her lauding as Great Fecund and her subjugation as worthless dirt. Nature's taken a scraping and bashing for too long now; it will be a struggle to raise her back to rightful status. There are enough hearts of women beating about the planet that identify with this urge to rework travesty into triumph. They don't make the news, their work secret or consigned to the kook bin.

When I forayed on these acres, She was a lap whose dips and rises I roamed without fear. Mom would guard me. She was a force and a fact, the backdrop, the giver, the arranger of all things Pleasure. I easily found myself in crevasses, the land's ravines and creek-cuts, praising the icons of vagina, auditioning as a vessel in which to sprout a little life. My turn!

I'd heard of her Son: not the one among prophets braying law, but the lover and cyclic grain, the stag and the hermit aged to sagehood. I gave him a nod on my way to her, until we moved here, and he kept showing up. I didn't expect him to be a satyr leading me into deeper woods. Will he lead me astray? Or is he the impregnator, a whisperer into the heart of Asa?

Mother of soil and sap, chlorophyll and corn silks, hail to my ultimate apprenticeship with you. I wish to swell until my bellyskin shines and my navel is a funny oops on the hill of in-utero. What will it feel like? I should have tried by now—I am running late at thirty-eight—but the beloved is ready. Your beauty is a tract of sixty acres decked out lushly, the Wood Man a fleeting presence who smiles when he shows. I refer him to Asa, the one with seed finer than acorns.

What's the inside scoop on forging new life in the belly? Does awareness of the cargo infuse each moment? Does responsibility to sail in peace become difficult navigation? Must I show the bump of my glory to everyone? How sheltered were the moms of my childhood, persevering in their tent-dresses that covered the miracle from prying eyes that wished to hungrily consume it! How will I, always ejecting words to smokescreen my body, respond to the public fondling by so many a gaze?

Dearest Mother, Earth romanticized as the greatest giver, may I step into your shoes? May you midwife and guide me? Again, I pray I am not too old to join the ranks of womb-wills. Let there be lessons in these months of independent study. I will be a body, housing birth. I will join you in the red tent when I see another woman carrying her private payload as I, too, heave mine with the gravity of one tasked with species continuity. Human thread still unwinds on this planet, propagating. Not done yet.

4

Four months into the marriage, four months—that's all we had before Asa lost his Great Mother incarnate, the womb that tossed him into this world. She'd been sick for some time, but Asa could not face the inevitable.

She was his anchor, his touchstone, his tether to safety. I waited to take over that part of her job but never could qualify, and now the position would be permanently but inadequately filled by Dead Mom, Wronged Mom, on leave for the rest of Asa's life.

Wronged she was from the beginning while he watched, helpless. Losing Asa's birth father in a foreign country because the man had impulses that didn't fit marriage was her first hit. Back in the United States after divorce, she was seemingly saved by another proposal of marriage, but the new man turned demonic. What could she do? In her mind, nothing but stand up without tearing the whole edifice down. Their skirmishes began early.

Each night of his childhood after he and his brother went to bed, Asa's parents settled down to argue. Pops and Lorene took their places in the living room, never moved until midnight, never screamed or threw things. They fought in firm yet practiced tones, not a belligerent beat missed between lunge and reply. The accusations and damnations were pointedly personal, encompassed all time, and wore the lace of lethal poison. On our first visit as a married couple, they were still at it.

A new bride and painfully aware of it, I stretched out next to the silent Asa and asked how I was supposed to sleep through this? The house was compact, a short hallway between us and the boxing ring. Asa rose and retrieved a fan he switched to high; it drowned out the bickering.

In the morning, nothing was said. I had no idea if my witness of the fight fazed Asa at all. For *she* was still alive, she was Mom, she was breathing, and his nightly soundtrack from earliest memories—their volleys and parries—wasn't altered by a change in the spousal guard.

We drove to the site of his boyhood. I tried to see gratefully the geography that had nurtured him. But the high plains were a sparse layout compared to our land. Furthermore, despite the late-night sparring, I couldn't feel the verbal assaults and outright negation the son had taken from Pops growing up, when nowadays everyone was so polite to me, and Asa was the prodigal returned. The drive-through was a quick tour; the parents lived in town now. I never got out of the car, never walked the ground he'd inhabited while being groomed to leave it. Austere spires of the German Lutheran church loomed as we slowly traveled the gravel roads back to pavement. His love-hate relationship with all that transpired there was a paradox as unexamined as the atmosphere in his parents' house as the fighting began.

I was saved from listening to the two of them rip each other to shreds through the night, sound drowned fully by a simple fan. I learned then I was a gnat trapped in the dark indoors though words were congenial in the light of day. I was no visiting princess; I had to find a spot, next to the drone of a wind-machine while Asa snored, where I wouldn't be blown to nothingness.

≈

Pops and Asa's mom may have wondered if I'd stick around for more than a handful of years, a woman starkly unlike the locals and not adept at ingratiating myself. Then again, they knew in their hearts that Asa was free of them, living miles away and toiling with his mind instead of brawn. But given the emotional stew in which Asa had come of age, and what I imbibed as a sample earful, I felt the weight in the air of each of the rooms where the couple moved heavily. The sorrow was thick around the gold sofa where Lorene, as I called Asa's mother (managing adroitly not to call Pops by any name) sat most hours. It was also where she settled to receive her nightly punishments, the verbal lashings, and in her turn to lay her own disappointments bare.

She *saw* me, I could tell that. She welcomed me. Yet her speech due to stroke was labored, her focus moved often to the next cigarette that would ease her distress. I could feel her wanting to turn Asa over to me, and I appreciated it even as I knew he orbited her still. Her spells of lucidity were like that, blunt and instructive. But then, she and Asa had always talked. Talked, and talked.

It was striking, how apparent it was that Lorene was due for another stroke soon and it would be her last. When she died, the hole Asa inhabited was deep and solitary. We'd had four months of hot newlywed sex, romantic companionship, and rural homebuilding. One day's deep tragedy, when her stroke came without a warning, and that rhythm was forever altered. I marshalled forces, fully ready to support my husband, but I wasn't invited into the country of his grieving. What was my response to that?

I continued to salute the turkey vultures and roar with the running creek as Asa opted less and less for visits to the outbuildings. His grief became a slow move over time into the house, the recliner, the flickering screen of shallow stories and insipid commercials, a sinking that took months to grow deeper and darker. I could never have guessed my robust rabble-rouser, my warrior for the underdog, my weekend posthole-digging darling would finally shrink from the green world and opt for blinds drawn in a TV-screaming room thick with the shadows of calamity and loss.

5

Announcements from the biological clock swept every other plan aside.

Riptides from the body's command destroyed the shore of proud childlessness. Overtaken by womb hunger, womb a cavity I could not see or feel, like the womb I'd been pried from by forceps. Not on your life would I allow that when the tables turned. Such are the edicts of baby-hunger, a lovely yet terrifying obsession. Once upon a time, men voiced relief that I had no interest in making a brood. Now I did. As luck would have it, Asa wanted kids, too. He wanted them more after Lorene left.

But we didn't embrace in the nook where mayapples would rise to applaud what they'd intuited from below. There was no full moon shining down, no blanket on which to sprawl. Rocky dirt even nearest the house was a clump-fest with tall weeds hiding critters; the yard not entirely screened from the road, the man not prone to get naked outdoors. We didn't take the trouble to haul a mattress Up Top where the whole sky could get at us, as clouds stirred up a blessing.

Nor did we disturb the deer in their thick-dank lair, or brave the fear of snakes where a low, ancient fence made of stones without mortar lined the southern ridge. True, my fantasies lay all over the land, but what I wanted more was an infant to hold.

Too bad that even though I walked dangerously close to the road on summer solstice in the sheerest of gauze only—to be near the St. John's wort blooming, said to be a fertility enhancer—we didn't take things up a notch in the garden. I did suggest it. I never knew which interlude got egg and sperm together, but in truth I loved our bed as much as any sky or rough ground out there. The bedroom was cozy before we remodeled it to bring in the sunlight; we could always feel the land on the other side of a modest shield of plaster and lath.

It was only a month after Asa's mother died that I conceived. I was thirty-eight years old and told by many that of course that was not too old! But did they secretly wonder, as I did? We hustled off for a first visit to the midwife, Asa soaked in the accolades at work, and I rode the waves of not-morning sickness, but something else, akin to an acid trip.

I felt either oneness with all beings or sharp razor-cuts of fear to the psyche, deflated by writing myself notes about caring things people said or did, stuffing them in a drawer, and promising myself to read them the next time a tsunami hit. I savored each acid-high or acid-hell until the end came way too soon—six weeks after the positive test. The bleeding didn't stop. Hope wrenched out of its holder.

The midwife was an M.D. OB-GYN, famous in the state for championing the holistic approach. But it was a doctor close by we ran to when the sad news broke, and she looked at the sonogram gravely. She said that they were overcrowded momentarily, and could we go sit in a supply room? After agonized waiting, the doctor slipped into the room, pronounced the death knell amidst boxes of catheters and syringes. "So sorry, so sorry. Goodbye."

Few people can say they were there when a piece of glacier breaks into avalanche, but who hasn't watched one on film? I felt buried by frigid weight. My tears even felt cold. Asa was silent, clenched against any show of emotion.

How could this happen? Was I just too old for this? Was the Cosmic Mother telling me I was not worthy?

I was the womb, and I needed Asa to be there for me. I overlooked the blow this might have delivered him because my splintered mind couldn't handle it. Plus, I was the one who bellied up to the promise and emptied the loss. The would-be carrier. The vessel, the midlife mama wanting so badly just one extra chance to have what others had.

Asa had been emotionally boarded up since the death of his own mother. A baby was a chance for renewal. Blown, squandered. No one said *miscarriage* except me, trying to expunge the pain with the blatant word.

Try again.

≈

Eureka! The line on the stick appeared and pregnancy, the great salvation, filled the house with promise. This time I didn't go strange in the head. There was too much worry for a psychedelic frame of mind. All my spare time went into manufacturing calm. Meditation, hypnosis scripts, walks into the land. Asa tuned back in on the hope channel. We had spells of tentative bliss.

But again, only weeks in, the bleeding began that signaled another loss.

The midwife was out of town. Her clinic sent me to a doctor she contracted to be in charge in her absence. It was a hospital setting, and his answer was a D&C. At least I didn't have the excruciating cramps and clots, a mocking mini labor like last time. Merely a "procedure," groggy nothingness, then done.

Back to the midwife, who was incensed.

"That doctor wanted to D&C babies I ended up delivering!" she shot at me, as if I'd killed the baby myself. *What was I supposed to do?* I never asked her: she was charisma incarnate, a star in the baby-having business, and the daughter of local celebrities.

Should I have bled until her return? Mistrusted the one she left behind to trust? What could I think of her after her shrill induction of blame into my deepening grief?

On the topic of trying yet again: "Surely you must have a sixth sense," I wheedled. "You've done this for so long. You must intuit who's going to carry to term and who isn't."

She was just this side of hippie-dippy, so you could entertain this power in her. She moved like an arrow trailing long auburn hair from room to room, and when she sat to regard me, I felt the reverberation of her momentum, her utter immersion in her work in the humble but sturdy red brick house-clinic, sporting turrets for birthing rooms.

Her mouth made a straight line. Her face didn't look good. She wouldn't say a word.

Asa wanted to sue someone. *Her.* For misleading us. For abandoning us to a doctor she did not trust, who may have made a grave mistake. All my spare time went into trying to dissuade him from a lost cause. She was an icon. I'd been in one of those birthing rooms, standing attentive, when my cousin labored there many years ago. To revile the birth-goddess would be to revile all home birth, and we couldn't do that! I beseeched him to leave it alone.

This time there were no condolence cards. Our kind neighbor still crocheted little blankets for the momentous day, but who knew what to say? I walked the land with zombie steps and a heart pounding *why, why, why?*

Once more and let the third time be the charm.

Disappointment again. Eight weeks in.

The blood leak I hated to see. This time the tears were hot with the scourge of failure. It happened while Asa was at work, and I was immobile on the bed when he came home. I was contemplating the upcoming pain, feeling robbed, and I'd had enough.

It was nightfall and the red river between my legs was coursing stronger. I walked into the yard to touch the edge where it went wild. I gathered every ounce of will I had and prayed hard this time, to a Death Goddess. Her name was Hecate, and she was known in Greek mythology as a psychopomp: a spirit who guides souls of the dead across a liminal area to the otherworld.

I was unrestrained in my selfishness, but realistic. I didn't ask her to reverse the catastrophe; I just wanted a pain-free "delivery." It's not often talked about, the way miscarriage follows the same arc as labor, only quicker perhaps. Perhaps. But the pain in my belly during the first miscarriage far surpassed any monthly cramps I'd ever known. Standing at the cusp of ruin number three, I begged to bypass the sheer body-agony of it, at least that, and I promised this would be the end of the quest to be habitable to a new soul on its way here.

As if in a fairy tale, the wish was granted. It was like an easy period, a shedding of the womb like any other childless month, and not a stab nor tweak of pain. Not one.

I tried to share the miracle with Asa. But he had checked out. I studied his averted gaze but couldn't tell where he went. I was to learn the next day that he wouldn't honor the bargain I made with Hecate, with myself.

After weeks of harsh words and tears and finally wanting to please and beat the odds, I caved, got pregnant, and miscarried again. This time, husband and thwarted dad lay on the bed with me during "labor." But he was in no mood to be sweet. We quarreled while it hurt, as it had the first time, for I felt too small and wrong to petition Hecate again. And just as I was reaching the crescendo,

Asa called me a name, rose from the bed, and strode out of the room.

≈

I tried not to make a connection between the nightly marital battles my husband grew up with and how things started to slip between us. I wanted to believe after Lorene's death that mourning was a pilgrimage with an end point, that healing would prevail. Home from the high plains and trying to banish the sad and skirmish-worn couple from my mind, I had questions to put to the woods.

Deep into marriage, things come out of the sticky air. All hail the challenge of learning what to live with. The slow filming over of bliss through unpredictable increments of time can fool one. With Asa it morphed from sprinkled quirks into a disposition. Before long I realized he was not so much obsessed with details but withdrawn from immediacy. His was an inward turning, not meditative but numb, as if to shut out the world. I urged him to slay grief for our sakes, but it was too soon. He had to try to turn us into *his* parents.

How it is that a marriage becomes tortured, a daily travail of wondering who will anger whom and how badly it will hurt? By what method does your man become a sullied jewel, once aglow not for his knighthood but for those rare qualities that bypass social conditioning and biological drives, subsuming the noise of gender difference and the mandates of lust? Where go open disclosure and empathy? When these evaporate, why must a woman rely on quoting her volumes of dissatisfaction, keeping up the dirge as if a perfectly tuned ear will someday hear, and how can a man not become bowed and appalled, or turn into a cur as if entitled to bite?

My beloved: so blond, so handsome, such softness of beard and strength of legs! Once attentive, once readable as a book and an avid reader of me, so sure, as I was sure, that *this* marriage would work. We craved *One Who Would Wipe Clean the Past.* Make everything better from now to forever. Up to this point I may have been a bumbler but look! Look at my fine man! The house, the land! Take that, you betrayers and deserters.

Yet Asa's mother deserted him, and emotionally he deserted me. Next came the hyper-sensitivity neither was ready for. We called it *flinching* at first, characterizing the misunderstandings and flare-ups as replays of bad old times with other lovers. That worked well until memories of the others faded, and they faded fast. Midlife marriage packs baggage that contains worn but comfortably held knives, old manuals on one-upmanship, and shadows who show up because the grief doesn't fade without diligent application. We fought over the stupidest things.

Words are the tip ends of pain; they're all we own sometimes. At first, they sprouted like intruders, easily weeded between Asa and me, the potent pesticide *I'm Sorry* very effective. The words among us that deflated love, one micro-puncture at a time, were shy on content. Content could be about a stopped drain or the light bill. Content was trivial, but we bit the hook, due to the subliminal shot, also known as what we thought we heard:

Do it my way or you're brainless/worthless.
You don't listen.

And the next level down:

Asa: *You must not leave me no matter what!*

Me: *Don't destroy my freedom with your vitriol! Don't turn us into Pops and Lorene!*

I wonder if all chronic marital fights come down to the fear of death. For Asa, my leaving equaled annihilation, yet holding me at arm's length was, in effect, his absence. For me, the words among us were soul-murder. At the point where tensions floated daily, I knew that without a break from consuming resentment, I was drifting toward a stress-related disease.

Fear of abandonment, fear of engulfment. Either way, is it a fear of not being? I began to think that Pops and Lorene were lucky:

at least they had truce in the light of day, and the time for shooting to kill was at a known hour, bracketed by ritual and rules. For Asa and me, conflict could erupt anywhere, anytime.

Work—my husband's sword and refuge—always got in the way. Or it saved us from all-out war. The cycle of battle and retreat continued.

Asa labored to have people pay him money for his thoughts, his strategies, and do for them accordingly. The law involved employing a crystal ball, game plans, and chutzpah. Lawyers should be warriors for the truth, or the cleverest at bending it. But Asa could never lawyer me during our strained discussions, and we both took solace in that.

I stood on a singular sideline where I could see him but no one else could. I couldn't tell them about authentic-him, living-in-terror him, unable to relax or sleep, the warrior that was brusque and barely civil to his mate. Asa needed to wear that lawyer mantle of authority, or our household didn't run, the land would be irrelevant, and the structures we built, both concrete and subtle, would be swept away in crushing debt and foreclosure. Without his work, and the wide, trusting eyes his clients held up to him, Asa was a sad boy crying on the stoop for his mom who would never return.

Before long, one thing that had drawn me with such interest— his utter devotion to knowing what he wanted to do in life, his passion for the law—turned to disgust. I was sorry to see it go. I gave up my therapy clients without regrets; I wanted to be a helper and a healer, but at midlife the role lost its warmth, its continuity, its ability to keep me growing. I needed the school that the land afforded, and I needed it badly. The yen for the land as a partner I could hear, touch, and see wasn't ranked higher or lower than the biological mom-urge: it was different. It was an undergirding. I hadn't been able to envision myself as a town-mom, wedged in among the cacophony of lives going full blast up and down street after street. I told myself I would be a better healer after taking this course upon the land pedagogic.

But despite his attachment to work, Asa demeaned his profession in dark moments. "Smoke and mirrors," he said, "that's my game, and people seem to go for it." He liked to mime the way he'd dramatically roll his eyes at the words of opposing counsel, or slam down a sheath of files on his table before rising to address the bench in indignation.

Professionally, we had both opted for words as tools and had no compunction at seeing the other as a competitor in their use. The words among us—well-crafted and deadlier than Pops' and Lorene's—were born from the loss of hopes accumulated at a crossroads stage of life. You lose lovers, then a parent, and finally four miscarriages come and go from the womb that promised redemption—how long can the soul hold up without letting the heart break utterly? You muster a bit of gung-ho for the usual stuff: money, accolades, property—but having them comes with no staying power. You never address anything that hurt, you just keep buying—but unnamed monsters are below the surface. Charge on, big man. Weep and rage, slighted woman. But never dare to dream yourselves off the treadmill. It could mean a step onto permanently scorched earth.

Sitting in the circle amid my rocks, I considered the impasse. Asa loved his dead mother more than me. He loved his work more than me, though his work would be his undoing. He failed to love his work with respect, with gratitude: he worried, he mulled, he flimmed and he flammed as paid to do. How could I effectively respond? I knew the size of the mortgage payment. But I fell deeper in love with cumulus towers or the cinquefoil's tiniest bloom, caught wanting a place to revel and hide, not sure that needing it was healthy, not sure it wasn't the high road after all.

That I lost embryo after embryo in the early weeks of four pregnancies would always mark us. I could not make it up to Asa, who blamed me covertly, and we drifted further apart. The sniping was a sad refuge that took the place of talk about a dead mom or kids who should have been toddlers by now.

If looks can kill, words can insert slow poison. Asa and I kept it up, with words that on occasion we admitted *wanted* to tear down walls, but only bricked them higher. We did it within earshot of others, and they cringed, so we stopped seeing others. What of the land? The land told me, *work it out among yourselves.*

But you! I pleaded. *Can I come to you whenever I can?*

Where was my man-spirit all hairy below the waist, the tree-bark eyes and buck scent rubbing? He was everywhere, but I looked away from him. Increasingly he was not a figure that could incite me to sensuous daydream in the presence of trees. I started going for walks too often dimmed by bitterness, laced with panic. It was all I could do to throw myself on the ground and wait until I felt the wind stroke my back.

6

Asa and I were of the same mind: turn to the labor of adoption, try for the youngest babies that could be at hand. Facing mounds of paperwork and soul-destroying scrutiny, we were criminals who had to recant and prove our worth. We still lived for a future, even though hope was thin-glimmered. Asa had sent his spirit to the next world with Lorene, and I could only lie still in the circle and breathe.

The visitor was tall and lanky and as uncomfortable as we were, but he covered it with a stab at superiority. He was the social worker sent to conduct a home-study to launch our efforts to adopt. I swear he could divine the acrid scent of lingering loss, and the desperation with which we looked to him to save us. Maybe he needed a buffer from the pity that welled within. Probably he was simply burned out by a job with occasional rewards, but too much awkward hoop-setting in these first few hours.

The hours of inquiry: were we fit to be parents? We put on our best show, believing it. Miscarriages were a badge that should obtain clemency and confer access, right? We had tried for a baby so hard.

He listened and wrote down every word we said. He asked what first attracted me to Asa. I gushed over my husband's gentleness and kindness and believed every word. Asa answered a similar query with notes about my verve and creativity. We were looking solid at that point. I believed we both believed the words among us that stung and sputtered could be trounced by the entry of a third soul with their blank slate in tow.

The social worker looked around. To describe our home, what would we call the style? Asa and I looked at each other, stumped, scared. His gaze caught us with sarcastic lips: "Eclectic?"

Oh no! Why couldn't I be more of an interior decorator? Why wasn't I like my mom, who chose her home's keynote with allegiance: Early American. How she collected pieces with pride and hewed to the theme. Asa and I blended furniture and belongings from other lives when we married, and as for the rest we were guilty of mixing cost considerations with spontaneity. Then there were the rocks and pieces of wood I'd collected outdoors, piled onto nearly every available surface, a plebian clutter to a man of taste. I had failed as a womb-host already. Now was my home not elegant enough to raise a child?

Later Asa said not to worry about it—the guy was gay. "You know how they are about furnishings."

My husband and I bonded over the inequity of it all. He referred to the penchant of the locals, for whom having babies was a fervent pastime, and how he often saw the parents later in court when their rights were terminated. We discussed teen pregnancy. We chewed over the world's burgeoning population, and how it seemed prudent to only replace yourself, popping out one apiece for you and your partner, and why wasn't there a law that mandated such a limit? Why wasn't every prospective parent grilled like we were? Why did we have to sit there like we were on trial?

We sweated the weeks of waiting, but voila, passed the test. We were fit enough to adopt.

Then more waiting.

Waiting for me meant grieving on the land. One day I invited them in, all four of them, the spirits who'd checked out this womb then had to leave. I couldn't make heads or tails of the why, but I wanted them to know they were always and forever welcome here. *Go as deep into the land as you want. And stay.*

There was one tree I called Grandfather that stood at the edge where the creek left our property for the neighbors.' It rose gallantly with feet in the water, bearing the barbed wire of boundary-making that someone nailed to its backside. Save a fencepost, pierce a tree. But Grandfather didn't bleed, as I had over and over. He listened well.

The land erotic babysat my grief, even when I told it I now hated sex. And I would never feel sexual again. Asa had pushed me too far—four miscarriages, the last one ending so badly, him grinding the heel of his boot into my soul just as the clot that could have been life was leaving. "Womb!" I said out loud, "I hate the word. It's archaic and dumb sounding anyway. I have one, and what good did it do? Now we pay good money and pirouette smartly to bring a child into our house."

The fees were hefty, and the stigma of not being a Birth Mom hovered like smog waiting for the huff of prevailing winds. Even after the babies came and the poisoned air of loss dispersed, it always surprised me how many onlookers would find themselves duty-bound to cough up an opinion about the daughters not being our *real* daughters.

Shadows, Romp Around

S unlit clearing made by subtle erosion—where the creek holds an oak so close you can lean against its trunk and stretch feet to clear water—I pray you become their haven: the spirits that didn't make it here into baby bodies.

I pray they see how, before the hill turns steep upward, a fresh batch of sky sparkles into this clearing—a playground if ever there was one. Let's be happy here.

This is for me, too. Allow my magical thinking to hover over shallow water with flat easy banks from which I imagine they will leap delightedly, those wraith-children. Allow me to call the towering tree Grandfather, a guardian for them, a protector that stands close, someone when I'm not here to watch over them. Let me designate this the perfect playground for them, because all four tried their best.

Spirits who had to move on, my wish is that you know you're welcome here. I did not banish you. I don't know what's wrong with my body that it couldn't make habitable space. I wanted you each time. So, I won't park my grief in this coppice, although you likely don't ascribe to the world's edict about where grief belongs (silent, unspoken) anyway.

I'll make it a little spot where we can talk. I release you by remembering you and let go of a burden for me. Gratefully, it's a draught of joy to call this your play-space.

Dear spirits of the ones who would come, I knew not your whys or wiles. They say that before our births we fashion a contract specific to the soul's aims. Were you just helping me out? Helping me to see that for once I don't get everything I want? Were you giving me a mystery to contemplate, was there a point?

I have not missed anyone I never met so much as all of you.

But if you could find some jollity here, picnic on giggles and marvel at the tadpoles. Once I was first choice on your trajectory to this corporeal classroom, from womb to adventures grand and small. Romp now in this great school, the land compatriotic.

At last, there were two more to learn of the land, each arriving in quick succession— infant girls. It was a time of redemption; Asa and I came into our own. Older parents marooned on a rural route, we didn't have peers in this venture. People found it amusing or occasionally insane as we raised babies in our forties. We two clung as conspirators to the adventure, and the harsh words between us receded.

The land lay in a conservative zone of small towns expanding and small farms giving up. Our gracious neighbor bestowed all the collected baby blankets she'd held onto, and with her husband, she embraced us and our girls. We navigated parenthood with our own surviving parents too old to lend a hand.

When you're baby-starved, with only the stamina to let children empty what's left of you, their advent is easy ecstasy. Enter their oblivion to the pettiness of your concerns about anything but their needy selves. Marvel at their blazing lack of guile, their mindfulness to a vivid cast of objects, goofy sounds, and mushed sustenance. You and the other adult in this conspiracy get to relive being new, and seeing it all through shared eyes, you two hold the same secret: *them.*

As toddlers, both were difficult. Who said girls are a gentler task? The oldest moved too slowly toward language, the youngest was loud and wild. Asa and I slipped on noxious words again, engaged in sharp tones against one another, and we did it in front of the little girls as if they couldn't hear—until brought up short by the looks on their faces.

As easily as we fell into it, we quit. Cold turkey. The words among us exiled for the good of the innocents, an opportunity to think outside the marriage box. Neither of us had raised children before—there were no applicable flinches to contend with.

Although not long for midlife's middle, I was in love with the newcomers and the whole endeavor of their care, fueled by the chance to guide and create not just nurturance, but pathways to raise better people for the planet. By toddlerhood, the revelation of the eldest's autism diagnosis was grist for the mill; I bore down into the hope of certain recovery with approaches that abated the affliction at first. Asa worked hard at his career and made such things as the private school and the behavioral therapies happen. When I claimed my breaks, I went to the land. It was of a piece then with the house, the parenting, the recovery of beautiful waywardness, and the chance to let the family work a different magic into my battered spirit.

Right quick it didn't matter that the girl-babies never began in my belly. I forgot that hunger with glee, glad to discover the essences of the adopted bairns day after day, glad to have them on the outside of my skin, charging toward their growth with grabby wills and incoherent yelling.

Still, I had my affair with the land, more private than ever. I was more tired than ever because one daughter didn't sleep well, but I was a servant to both their needs. I was someone at last: another speck of mirror image to Earth as Mother, a chip off the old block as wide and big as our planet. She let me rest on her bosom in any kind of weather.

Babies Rule, Praise Up Top

Praise the oaks whose acorns I rob by the handfuls for an altar indoors.

Praise the incidental furniture where I rest on my way Up Top, an ottoman of rock beside ruts long ago a makeshift road.

Praise the deer that skitter at the edge of my pausing to think while availed of this rock.

Praise the creek where rains over slight boulders make glassy rumps that must appear like Niagara Falls to small feeders.

Praise the wild strawberries and plums I wish for the patience to gather.

Praise cedar for its ballroom gowns spread across the quietude and praise the nerve of evergreen juniper nipples.

Praise the tallgrass that has taken back this flatland from alfalfa, the goldenrod and black-eyed Sues, the place we buried our elder dog.

Praise the breath-woven tether that loops my sight and listens to the long wind down the hill and through the orchard to the house, where new circumstances bid for peace and plenty.

Praise the private nature of this enterprise, the return of the loving man, the innocence of the watchful infants who have taken us from our malaise.

7

The first daughter Asa and I welcomed knew wind or leaf to be as fascinating as any toy in the corner of her crib. I carried Nina everywhere—through the yard, to the circle, although the climb Up Top and the creek's rocks were too rugged for an infant in arms. Later she thrilled to the swing launched from her dad's hands, sat in the wading pool as a lover of water, stood among the scratching chickens. They duly accepted her odd gestures. We had her diagnosis by then—autism—but she still ran outside with glee. When, how, and why did she turn, not just aside, but downright aversive to the out of doors?

Pets were the first casualty. "No dog!" she demanded, and the sweet boy turned tail with a sadness he could not hide. Maybe Nature was too vast without walls, replete with changes in weather that rendered light and sky never the same reliable sameness. Or was it because I stopped trying to overcome her protests at the sight of crawdads in the creek and rocks with moss hair? I gave up—too soon?—with her distress obvious, her wishes clear. She was seven, eight. "No creek!" she screeched. "Back to the house!" Nina's hasty beeline for enclosure said it all.

The chaos of autism structured life tightly with its behaviorist routines. To the far back burner of mind, I pushed Asa's quirky OCD traits, for they were nothing compared to this. I'd held hope that maybe her disorder would fade in the pure truth of the land itself, that the daughter would overcome just as I had steadied myself there. It was not in her cards.

The mishmash of guilt, loss, and savor inside me did a Mobius twist. The land would be *all* mine, the loss that she and I might share it turned into one more grief to place on the altar. I would not force a person into a sensory experience that damaged their day so strenuously. But also, I would be free: of the vigilance, the role, the responsibility of overseeing another's time in the natural world. I escaped the pressure to surrender the land to a wholesome family romp and hid my body's cry to focus squarely on myself.

≈

The youngest was a different if plucky girl, in love with Disney movies and pretty dresses, kittens and cooking, before she got tough to survive her peers. She'd been a happy baby, a rough-and-ready toddler, and she navigated her girlhood with a confidence that made us wonder if those unknown birthparents could after all bequeath such things as will and fearlessness.

One afternoon Asa came home earlier than usual. We sat in the den looking onto the circular driveway. We watched Sierra trailing a stick, looking away from the house, walking slowly, down the lower curve only four feet from the wild. Long dark hair sweeping her back, small in stature, muscular and strong, simple friends with sun and rain. It was the nature of her focus and drawn-out pensive stroll that held us—she, the one usually in fast motion, purposeful, joyous dancer and intrepid tree climber.

She sauntered and stared into the woods—not where I roamed, but the hollow between our house and the neighbor's winding drive, leading to their place on a high hill none of us had ever seen. She twirled her rough stick absent-mindedly, like a baton, then poked the gravel driveway with it as if it was a cane. She paused to face that nearby bowl of woods. She walked, then paused again. And again.

Sierra no longer asked to accompany me when I hightailed it out. She knew the phrase, "Break time for Mom!" and could see through me to weariness, need, my love for what lay beyond. How she managed my hunger to be alone, I couldn't tell.

Asa and I continued to sit like blobs in armchairs. We knew her shoes were scuffed and knees skinned from adventures in the yard as per every day. Her hair wore tangles at the ends; she wouldn't hear of a ponytail. When I saw her musing out there, I hoped it was a little chip off my Nature-loving block but knew better. There was no way to absorb her into myself, this puzzle of practicality and vulnerability. I could only step around for fear of warping her by revealing the true extent of my distraction, my unnatural devotion to the land erotic.

Her reverie struck us stranger by the moment, seeing her sustain a pace like that, a kid who charged through life stopping only to cry over *Beauty and the Beast*. Watching her in low gear for once in her life, I held my breath.

The television news chattered but Asa and I craned our necks to see the driveway curve again. Was she unhappy? Sierra was the one who made the family look good. Gregarious and well-liked by other children and adults, comforted by a bed full of stuffed animals in the rare moments she cried, every day was a new nut to crack.

We were relieved that she took the spotlight from the afflicted one, the one who invoked questions about demeanor and behavior from kids who were blunt, and from adults who equated autism with retardation. Asa and I didn't care for scrutiny either—not as parents, older parents, isolated parents, special-needs parents. In a way that we'd never admit out loud, the youngest anchored all of us to okay-ness.

How did she do it? How did Sierra maintain the cheer and open heart to greet the world with a bounce from bed to firm feet on the ground, grabbing life with all senses cocked for the on-slaught? How did she escape the currents in the house that clashed when one came around corners? How did she see beyond parents sitting in recliners with bodies like rocks lifted artificially from their native tumble, plopped onto fabric as display items meant to pass for something fully unencumbered?

Does it give the lie to the supposition that Nina, locked into herself while the house churned around her, felt only pain? That the years of caring adults knocking to get in, to show her real life beyond the tragedy of the autism epidemic—these mattered? Could she learn the lesson of how love and patience connect by how we wrapped her in our arms and plied her with words that described the world, made of the world a thing of enticement, so that she might reach in and reach back. Could it be working?

Did each one of these daughters, then, come with their own mission, by looks diametrically opposed, and yet who am I to ladle pity on one hand and gratitude on the other? Sierra coming up the driveway reassured me of one thing: she, the invincible, was going to be all right.

Eventually the girl circled back to the house, with fewer long looks at the hill. Then the door opened, and Asa had to ask, casual but expecting the goods, for she was no concealer yet:

"What were you doing out there?"

The answer came from the side of her mouth as she went breezing by, her mind on the next thing and not even bothering to look at us. One second before sound, we knew it would be at once profound yet no big deal. She tossed the words without a glance at our searching eyes.

"Just looking at my land."

She was seven years old.

I knew then there was a sequence she intuited, a thread of green we would hand her: the soul of her land as hallowed by her mother, who hid out in the trees and cavorted with silence, as an off-duty parent's pleasure beyond the house. The literal key to the place would come from her father, whose profession enabled our home and free passage throughout the land ancestral.

But what portion of that land would Nina get? As time passed, I failed to see how she could grow up and live alone in the country when we were gone. I couldn't ask Sierra—even begin to intimate it as a possibility for her adulthood—to orient her life around her sister's needs. At least Asa and I were lucky enough to be united for Nina's recovery. The stats about autism parents whose marriages end in divorce are damning. I *believed* we were united. I didn't ask what Asa thought, as long as he continued to pay for her therapies, caregivers, and expensive diet and supplements. Supporting her materially he was committed to; but I suppressed the sore space in my heart most days about how early and enduringly he gave up on trying to understand her.

Asa began to pull away from Nina emotionally. His attention and starry-eyed love for his first child seemed to halt on a dime. She was only a toddler; how could I explain that to her? I hoped that my stepped-up efforts to reach her would compensate for Daddy's cold shoulder. The sad and befuddling irony was that he was a disability rights attorney, among various hats he wore. Later I met other neurotypicals who worked with people with disabilities but couldn't tolerate them in their free time.

I could understand him on one count: it was a big shift in our lives. First his mama dies, then the miscarriages, then this. How much can a man withstand? One who lets persons detail their laments, one who then stands and speaks for them in court, one who visits the jail, sometimes six days a week? He had *nothing left to give*, he said, over and over. Though periodically he tried: dropping Sierra off at her events, he would ride around with Nina listening to baseball on the car radio, which somehow calmed her, buying her peanuts at the gas station since peanuts she adored. Putting her to bed on those rare nights I ventured out, freed, I could tell by how she described "daddy put you to bed" (pronouns were a puzzle to her) as Asa allowed himself to be at ease without me hovering, instructing, ready to give a grade of Pass or Fail.

Nina's care fell to me, but autism didn't wreck us. It's not like I was dying to get back into the workaday world; I wanted to parent, and I put my shoulder to the wheel, always taking Nina's recovery for granted. She'd get there. No, Asa's pattern of checking out was already established, and I was its first recipient when Lorene went away. That he could turn aside from the adoring eyes of a preverbal child though, this was hard to forgive. But it wasn't the *only* hard-luck factor driving me to the land that was never neurotic.

8

Bliss slips and falls in tiny steps until the bruises cover you. Children grow and we forget their miraculous beginnings. Asa traveled, and traveled some more, for work—I missed him, wanted him, needed him. He openly relished the trips as a breather. I was never invited, nor was a family vacation suggested to coincide with his hearings. When home for a stretch, he drove twenty miles to his satellite office in town simply to check email.

Asa talked about women in airports, hotels, shuttle-bus stations—how they beheld him. I had to believe he was steady on the fidelity point because if that broke, so would the whole edifice of our lives. Besides, he was uneasy with the role these women fashioned. "They want a father figure so bad," he mused. "One woman had to brush my hair—right in front of the boarding gate." (Asa's long ponytail gleamed against his white shirt and tie, a notable but attractive contrast. One doesn't easily and temptingly touch a stranger's hair in public.) "And every time I'm in Houston there's this same desk clerk who wants to be invited to my room. I tell her I have an early day tomorrow . . ."

But I knew the smile he could sustain, the eye contact held throughout the flirtation and how it would convince each one: *he wants me, he's just a good guy to his wife.* Women responded to Asa like that and often in front of me. I never piped up with the facts for them: *He would never speak to you the way he does so poisonously to me, so you see, as the prize winner my honor is dubious but yes, it is mine to keep.*

As the daughters moved through their elementary years, Asa needed ever more "space." It fell to me to be the caregiver, cook and bottle-washer, which wore thin, and I stood in complete amazement at him: such attestations of equal parenting in the beginning, such glad partnership when the girls were miniatures! What happened? Was it me driving him away, was it really autism with its slow progress for the stricken one, or were ghosts of his own childhood rising in livid anguish, begging him to hear and see?

Or had we fallen over a threshold that was too tremulous, pushed into unfamiliar territory by our bodies' advance to the downslide of age while we crafted a life most people attempt at the outset of adulthood?

≈

I came to the land's acres a mix of heretic and back-to-the-lander, with a fixation on family before it was too late to experience it. Thinking past "real estate" as a price-value, a pretty place, or a buffer wasn't something I could share with the neighbors who surrounded us. Where did I get the notion that conclaves of oak giving way to bluestem could hold teachings at once archaic, and, for the likes of me, utterly new?

From books and from groups of loosely organized souls looking for something that eluded us in every church or school. I sought these kindred spirits until I saw our poverty of focus, the way we were seekers when it suited us, the hungry ghosts inside our minds grasping for more. But it wasn't our fault. We didn't grow up with any orientation to earth, water, or sky except the false idea that they were inanimate, without sentience or rights, and ours to use. We longed to live as if they mattered tremendously and to abandon our roles as overpowering greed-sters by promising to be benevolent stewards. But where was the support for any of that? We were overrun by the whip-lashings to be *Achievers First and Saddled Possessors of Things.*

And yet. When the peace, lack of pressure, and aesthetic delight in Nature build to reach a crescendo, that impending leap is hard to resist. Mother Earth's lap is wide open, soft, and vast enough to break a fall. The land teaches basics of getting religion: parental protection from One so encompassing it can be envisaged as nothing but a safety net that never fails.

According to ancient texts, God the Father offers prophets and divine sons as his managers for the wildfire of devotion. The mostly male hierophants are super-humans to emulate, custodians of peace, and they are guaranteed deliverance but meanwhile, those icky people burn in hell. I couldn't stomach this view by the time I was fourteen, so I did what was the only sophisticated about-face at the time: deny ineffability, scorn true believers.

It wasn't until I was decades past my teenage-leftist loudmouth phase—proudly atheist and quick to despise religion as the "opiate of the people"—that I came across the entirety of that famous quote from Karl Marx upon which I'd fashioned my straw pony. It shattered me. I saw that I'd been duped into another finite set of beliefs that sought to hide the poetry, the ambivalence, the full spectrum—in order to ensnare followers and cast the enemy as clueless. In my youth I'd bought hook, line, and sinker the belief that communism could make real an educated utopia, while religion was for the less intellectual.

Marx's *full* "opiate of the people" comment disturbed my stultifying sleep about the need within us to explore a deep well with no name when I read the part most often left out: "religion is . . . the sigh of the oppressed, the heart of a heartless world, the soul of soulless conditions."

What is sacred desire versus the consumer's hanker for new glitz? When is it time to sit tight and love what is? The children were foremost, along with the task of trying simultaneously to live with Asa's increasing emotional distance and still be a loving if embattled partner. The land erotic didn't cease to blow kisses or deny its thoroughly sensual self. Definitions of that juiciness were shifting though.

What I was determined to ignore was the body's say in all of this. Mine was a body besieged by stress, a stress ameliorated by loving connections. These connections obscured the march past my own sexual prime. I fell back on Mother Earth because I had no human guide on this foray into what the tagline "householder" meant for a would-be mystic with her own acres to swirl in, a landing-zone for God-Gods-Goddess-All, the heart in this heartless world. What I hadn't bargained on was the Man of the Woods with his dangerous lessons, the call to Lover Earth.

Some days we are sexually charged for action in the flesh, hands lips and erectile tissue fortunate enough to meet the same in the beloved. Some days we might transmute that fire into creative work, or other days simply be willing to sail on our busy way and say, *Well hello there, my erogenous zones, nice to see you alive and well.* What happened to the Wood Man who pulled taut all the erotic surge I could take in from rocky soil to ponderous cloud, gave it human if hairy and feral form, and offered it to me? I think he was just passing through. During stolen tendrils of time spent staring into the creek, I missed him. If he could send a postcard, it would read: *There are no rules, no borders between what I showed you and how the Mother holds you.*

Pray Naked

E cosex, eco-sex, ecosexuality. The concept flashed in the pan, a good argument forsaken, ascribed to titillation, a book and some theories dismissed. Sexecology or the greening of sex: the way such phrases are devoured into disuse, discarded by the shamed who sneer to the left and right. But if you have passion, why hide it in the bedroom? Why hide the flesh and obsess endlessly about it? Go naked in the woods, watch suffering diminish. Then pray:

Please, holy haven, bring away the stranger I am to myself, vulnerable and gauche without the cloth sheath. Remove these scraps of tailored fabric. But I might get scratched, sunburned, or goosed by a branch! I am so scared to shed my layers with you. I cling to my responsibilities and the fortress of home so I can call myself a completed work. Is it enough?

How sex and prayer reverberate with their reach out and reach in: we know when we love, when we tantra, when boundaries dissolve before the commingling gets cerebral. It is then we know that sex, the act, is a prayer. But in too deep comes the recrimination, the flinching, the fear, and it's all about orgasm, the localized prize. Whatever happened to multi-level bliss? You tempted it with narrative, silly.

I could have been a connoisseur, dipping from erect phallus to phallus, a bee-buzz sex addict drunk on now this one, then the next. Damn the hard wiring and the old useless argument: are we humans monogamous or polyamorous? Out in the land erotic, I can have sex with anyone. Any hello that attracts me. Truly little of it is physical, yet most encounters are a whole-body wave.

I pray to be seen. Clothing or no-clothing is irrelevant. I pray to be one with You . . . shall I call you Earth? My land? So possessive, but I love it. What it really means is that I am yours, not the other way around.

I pray for beauty. I pray for the serenity of being held without demands. I pray for the freedom that I obtain, unseen on this cordoned-off paradise. I pray for what I already have. Not a petition is this prayer, but a Glory Be. Hail shagbark hickory and common wild carrot, hail the tiniest sparkle poured over belly-size rocks by the rain becoming creek epitomizing *flow*.

Our thoughts, mine and those of the land with mysterious cognitions, are each other's. To them I beam gladly: I will not harm you, and this you must see in my eyes—or some point where motivations coagulate, maybe the pineal? Another organ on an array of aural wheels that link the sacrum to solar plexus, the will to the heart, then rise through the wise eye and finally the crown you wear where we link, the top of my head coming off in a clean break.

9

In the circle I often thought about my bloodline, back to those who lived in tighter communion with Nature. I'd explored genealogy, relatives I barely missed knowing: farmers, pharmacists, lawyers, suicides. But those across the great ocean, the great-great-great-grands and backwards to indigenous generations—I fervently wished to know how these ancestors lived before the land stopped telling its secrets in their native tongues.

I fixated on Ireland, country of my mother's folk. Its scent of magic has long been sung, even exploited, but that doesn't change history. Christianity did an amiable dance with the natives when it arrived, only burning a dozen persons as witches over five hundred years while the rest of Europe smoldered.

But my bloodlines range all over the continent. I'm mishmash, clueless about what my ancestors did before agriculture and professions. Another white person lost in time, with no inherent knowledge to speak for the land—feeling the giant hole left behind.

≈

Asa despised the work of genealogy, reviling those who spent precious time on such pursuits. I figured it was the sour father-root, for he was doubly wounded. Pops was a stepfather-adoption scene. His mother had loved the dashingly handsome biological father of Asa, one Arthur Winters, and in 1958 Arthur Winters had done her so wrong.

As newlyweds Lorene and Art traveled to Japan to teach English. It was an adventure beyond any their counterparts could imagine, facing their futures in a sea of wheat and cattle. But once abroad, Art fell into gay men's beds when there was no support anywhere in the world for LGBTQ+ out-comings. He also took to sharing needles full of hard stuff and couldn't stand to be near his toddler son. By the time Asa was three, mom and son were stateside, and the divorce was final.

But years passed and Arthur Winters re-sculpted his life, returning to America to teach high-school drama on the eastern seaboard. He wanted to know his son. The case went all the way to the state Supreme Court, but Mr. Winters lost. Years later he was mugged and killed in New York City. The assailant was never found. Once, overnight in the Big Apple for a hearing, Asa wandered the same area in a daze after darkness but escaped with only numbness where feeling and thought might have stirred.

Pops, savior of a divorcee and her little boy, failed Asa in short order as a cussing, criticizing boor that small-town merchants barely tolerated, some refusing to do business with the man. Pops quickly grasped the bond between mother and son and set out to air his grievances daily, while attempting to mash Asa's self-image into bloody pulp.

The much-mellowed Pops I knew was a small, rotund gnome with bad knees and a cardiologist. He went to his grave—Asa taking the pleasure to literally piss on the headstone—before our daughters made it to elementary school. My husband surprised me with the graveyard story after one of our trips to his old home-grounds to finalize some of Pops' affairs. A story of significant urination!

I pictured the cemetery and knew what measure of bravado goaded him to whip it out and point the flow onto that costly, chiseled marble. The town sat on wide open prairie; the graveyard outside city limits sported not a single tree, hedge, or gazebo to break up horizons in any direction. Headstones bumped or laid flat inside a fenced area, just a brief stroll from the church with its severe German architecture. "Nobody was there!" Asa replied to my incredulous face. "Not a car was in sight. The rectory is too far away for anyone to see a thing, plus I turned my back to it. Don't look so surprised!"

I tried to collect myself because I grasped what an accomplishment this was on his part. I could only hope the long suppression of his rage in simmering silence was transformed and released. "I'm glad you did it! I bet it felt great!" I gushed. But I wanted to know more. "Did you . . . say any words?"

"It was kind of like a ritual," Asa smiled. He knew little about ritual beyond the Lutheran rites he'd rejected for years, or the euphoria gained among thousands crowding a stadium to share some focused, heady hours urging on their team. But I was intrigued that he made the most of showering the grave with raw fervor at last.

"So yeah, I said a few words. Beginning with, 'take *that!* Take that for turning me into your rival for my mother when I wasn't even in kindergarten. For never coming to any of my school activities, for making fun of me when I had that heart infection and got fat, for going the extra mile for your bloodline son but also for making him a nervous wreck. Your bad fucking attitude every livelong day but Sunday, and only part of that day—your nonstop preaching the gospel according to you, and how we, but not you, were going to Hell!"

He wasn't finished.

"And for what you did to Mom, you dumb farmer. Decades of putting her down. You quit paying her health insurance only months before her stroke; you didn't pay for therapy afterwards. You stinking son of a bitch! She might have been alive today. She never got to see my daughters."

I thought he was going to cry, but Asa turned and said, "and all the while I'm still peeing while saying this—lots of coffee that morning."

It was a fitting micturition, and Asa saw that I approved. I hoped it helped; it also helped me to put the matter of Pops to rest, full of hope that the son could at last move into his own without the shadow of the nay-sayer lurking. But after this event, Asa became even more quiet about his past, still bat-out-of-hell intent on his work. Keeping ahead was paramount, ahead of the prophecy Pops instilled—that Asa would never amount to anything. It was easier to piss away the memories of Pop's terrible acts than to defeat this underlying judgement of the son's soul. I thought more about Asa's birth father, because the face I looked at every day reprised the utterly handsome Arthur Winters. Asa never stopped hating either of his fathers, never ceased dumping scorn on such travesties as genealogy and family reunions. He asserted that he didn't want to meet either one of them in the afterlife either!

I mulled the details of Asa's origins because it might offer a way to save him, save us. I was also, admittedly, drawn to the pathos of the tale.

The scandal of Art and Lorene was unmentionable among Asa's extended family. There was no acknowledgement of the ordeal, no ceremony of healing for Asa and his mother, no one to safeguard the stories with patient airing, settling them into the family archive with forgiveness and consensual forgetfulness. *Art went gay and drug-addict overseas* was the extent of it in late 1950s Midwestern understanding. Lorene was somehow both victim and guilty party for letting her man go unspeakably astray. The new man in their midst would be her savior and an instant "Pops."

We flail, bury only to excavate, and wrestle the past, sadly situated in family pain-triangles, left with only psychology to unravel these mysteries. Therapy pledges to seek revelations but ends up charting our deviations. It gleams as a rational haven where people are either crazy or they are not. I looked to its secular worldview to make sense of the ways life rips us apart. The more I learned from the land, the more I found psychology threadbare. But I remained under the spell of its promises and nomenclature.

Sometimes I think therapy rose to referee language from the heart's murderous intent, by revealing the luminous function of what's hidden in our lives. Other times I think it's easier to affix a diagnosis, to brand people so we know how to access a blueprint for controlling them. How many ex-lovers decry their former squeeze as authentically insane? How many parents surrender their children to facilities and wash their hands of them?

If we look past therapy's penchant for pushing pills or palaver, then naming stands as its greatest power. To name a fault-line in one's character suggests it can be gentled, matched to a plan for the goal—losing the size and shape of it for good.

In time I found a descriptor for Asa that fit like a glove. But the prognosis was not hopeful. The term became the ultimate in words-among-us—Asa understood the moniker from clients and court records, and I used it without restraint. It packed a punch way beyond the half-joking jab of OCD. What a relief to claim a fitting phrase when there was no other root to hold onto.

Enter the experts on borderline personality disorder. I held my beloved up to that clinical light—his unending anxieties and little rituals seemed in service to some larger malaise. What to call the charming person who navigates the world of work with panache, but leaves permanent scars on his or her family?

And of course, there is that three-letter (always three!) shorthand for the disorder: BPD.

Having a framework to finally explain someone else is a fleeting relaxation technique. It's also a tool of desperate power. I found the diagnosis of BPD and its literature to be a minefield with tempting foliage hiding the surface. I wanted to pick each pertinent fruit evoking cries of "that is so true!" without having limbs blown off in the process. Because whenever I uncovered another symptom that fit Asa, the verdict of the experts hit hard: *untreatable. There is no cure.* What to do when you encounter the borderline male?

Run like hell.

But hell had closed off the exits. We had kids, a mortgage, and too many years into midlife to quit this last-chance dance. I fed Asa's fire with fire because tears humiliated me and were useless to him. It was my only defense, my feminist duty, my soul's cry to exist. Later, I cooled off my charred heart in the creek.

Since the multiple reasons why Asa and I put each other in crosshairs were irrelevant and the underlying accusations, with their familial precedents, too huge to handle, I looked instead for an organizing principle to interpret and hopefully reverse the damage done. Without Linnaeus and Lamarck to christen the living parts of our world, would we have completely lost Nature once the industrial revolution rolled over her? I needed a taxonomy of this marriage. I settled on borderline personality disorder because chaos dissected beats chaos archetypal, and in the fine points of BPD, my husband's faults took shape.

The experts were changing their tune. They said that no longer was the camp of crazy borderlines only inhabited by females who'd suffered sexual abuse. One-third, one-half of those tagged BPD, are men. Their human-to-human relationships are terribly conflicted. They are the classic *can't live with 'em, can't kill 'em* folks. All are survivors of parental abuse of some sort.

Asa's father did run a far-reaching reign of terror. Although son bonded with mom, she often checked out emotionally, drained dry by the lack of romantic love and the nightly marathon of killing words in the living room. Heartsick, Asa pleaded with her to get a divorce, but she feared poverty and stigma in rural western Kansas, circa 1964. She drilled it into him: flee from here, become a lawyer with a red sports car. He did as he was told, squeezing his client files and his frame into the chassis of a Datsun 240Z.

There was righteousness but also dread as I regarded core BPD symptoms. Why did it feel so familiar? Didn't everyone vacillate between fear and need, recognizing that to count on another human being was fraught with grave consequences? Who could fail to miss such an obvious and ordinary danger?

But there was the increase in Asa's free-floating and plaguing anxiety, absent only during our courtship. What's so unusual about a breadwinner in a demanding profession, also a father with a special-needs child, being stressed out? I fantasized Asa would quit the rat race, grow food and chop wood, blending with me into the land.

I could never get the jump on the chaos he seemed to need. It churned constantly, Asa juggling and struggling through our rocky marital atmosphere on top of dealing with some father-figure at work—and always the war with money, its frightful scarcity or beckoning sheen. I learned how the bank account was an arbiter of mood, thief of sleep, Asa's ship upon which wife and children were mere passengers, begrudged for being on board. It was Pops's "out in the field," all over again.

Another BPD trait is acting out after intimacy in the bedroom. Asa didn't stay long—he would be snack-hungry, or there was a television program, or it was too early to sleep. I got used to that. But like clockwork, a storm unleashed after we reunited from under the sheets, even if it was the next morning. I was in the doghouse for some peripheral misstep, the clouds of contempt dark and the acid rain from his tongue particularly toxic.

A bigtime post-coital cuddler, I beat my bitter retreat, but the thought did occur to me:

Run like hell.

10

Asa as the Borderline Male . . . or a timeless story of the one lost, but also the brave? I never outgrew my Greek-myths phase. Least interesting were the heroes, with one stellar exception: Odysseus. In the *Odyssey*, the main man stands out as the one most stricken by nuance, the type of character we come to stories for. I care less about his exploits in war than for the man doggedly trying to get home once the carnage was over. When I saw that Asa was living this myth, I understood the hero's wife, Penelope, struggling to keep the hearth fires burning against the odds of the lost but brave one's return.

Was my beloved a hero to me, despite the words among us, the sorrow-pierced childhoods we each labored through, the shame and the mistakes with their endless ripple effect? Can a married person stay for years, raise children, and surf the tides of income and possessions, share a bed, and hold enough heart-based moments despite losses and strife . . . and *not* be tempted to see the partner as heroic—even if you can't say it out loud? Without a nod to human myth and lore, no matter how unconscious, bonds shrivel. The living marriage becomes sick like a diseased organ or mind. There were many reasons Asa was larger than life to me, even though—to lunge a giant step away from the Greeks—the Four Horsemen of the Apocalypse were rife in our marriage.

Criticism, contempt, defensiveness, stonewalling—a marriage counselor's take on what kills love, despite those public promises of forever. Can these four poisons predict an uncoupling? When I brought this problem to Asa, he listened with the now-familiar weariness at what he feared were arrows to come. I insisted that we do these four things all the time.

"Doesn't everybody?" he countered.

We were both privy to the scandalous behavior of Asa's clients where post-divorce pandemonium stormed his office persistently. I wanted to think we were better than those people. I knew how Asa held himself above the hoi polloi that reviled their spouses and agonized for themselves across the table as he furiously scribbled notes. But had he given up on our marriage?

Why honor the heroic beneath countless doors slammed on discussion and intimacy? Because I knew the who-he-is dimension of Asa transcended the now-he-does, the real person revealed during courtship and the first stretch of marriage. If you can't suss out a hero in that stretch of time, you're not trying.

He worked for the poor and disabled, was smitten with animals, and always preferred mediation over litigation, but here was the kicker: he and his mom had been tight. She was a real-deal woman, snowed under by Asa's aggressive father, broken at last by spurs put to the Four Horsemen's rides until she had a stroke. She was left with speech a struggle, paralysis of limbs, mind trapped, and total disability. Still, the mother-son bond survived.

That is, until she took her last breath seated in the kitchen in front of us. She'd been revived once before by emergency medics, so this was expected. But without a doubt it was the worst moment of Asa's life. This time the medics couldn't save her. To make matters worse, the hospital unceremoniously placed her contorted body, dead on arrival, a leg lost to diabetes and toothless mouth wide open, on a bare steel table and said the family could go on in for a last goodbye. The image never left him.

It was after his mother's death that he took his ship to wander. I could no longer crawl on board, as it were; I held no special place. Did Asa have borderline personality disorder? Or was he tragically lost on foreign seas of grief?

Like Odysseus.

I warmed to the Greek man because he didn't want to go to war. He pulled out all the stops to avoid it, quite simply happy at home. Penelope and he had a new baby and he counted on the loving support of his elder parents rounding out the domestic arrangement. The new father didn't give a rat's ass about the fortifications of Troy or rescuing the beautiful Helen, who'd run off with some Trojan prince. Helen was his wife's cousin, but Penelope just rolled her eyes about the whole thing. Men were forever after Helen, and the golden girl made her choices freely, some of them plain stupid. This abduction was a welcome, hawkish spin on the part of the Greek men who fumed: Trojans were vermin to them, and vermin who enjoyed attention from a remarkable Greek woman were an excuse to strike.

I'm drawn to Penelope's strength. But was she as locked psychologically into the O-man as I was to Asa? That men are forced into work/duty is an old story, but at least Ody tried to pull a fast one. Prescient that he'd be pushed to lead some troops, Odysseus checked out his odds. An oracle said he wouldn't make it home for twenty years if he joined that fight. No way could he miss his comfortable sprawling house and productive farm that long! He had to do something to throw everybody off the trail, even though the king was fingering him for the job of commander.

The king sails to visit our hero and work on him a bit, with Odysseus' best friend in tow. The man of the house sees them coming from a high field and hatches a plan. Ody tethers his ox and donkey to a plow, puts a whacky cap on his head, fills his mouth with gravel and his sack with salt, then commences to plow backwards. *Poor man*, thinks the King upon approach: *he's gone insane.*

But Odysseus's BFF isn't so sure. Ody is known for cunning. His friend snatches the baby from the arms of a nursemaid and puts the infant directly in the path of the plow.

Penelope screams as Odysseus halts the animals an instant before the hooves trample. "Your tricks," the men remind him, "will not save you." Odysseus sets out with twelve ships for Troy. His fate was sealed, like Asa's, perhaps?

I don't think Asa realized what was being asked of him when he soldiered to the ship he could not avoid: the one where mom dies, and grief closes in like the forbidding walls of an alien city. A person can't trick their way out of experiencing the death of parent. The oracle has already spoken—you will lose them eventually. There will be trials finding your way back to normal. There isn't clarity in a period of mourning, especially one as lengthy as the wandering that Asa took to because he couldn't find solace in the affection of those who loved him.

Still, the Greek hero Odysseus made a choice: to go beat up on straw dogs knowing he might not make it back. Asa did too, because from his mother's funeral forward he dulled emotion, and sparring with me became his stressful but preferred pastime. Thus, the marriage began to spoil as my beloved went off to murder his feelings from within a high walled city, falling prey to the distractions of a pointless war. He took a few pleasant stops on the way back when the daughters were young, then got swept out to foreign seas without a single tool for navigation. Finally, when he wanted to come home, he would find himself unrecognizable.

Lorene, Please

ood day, silence. I hear words in my head, but I have come here to lose them, peeled from my brain as I exit the house. Some of them linger, so I give them tears for succor. I am so weary of fighting with my husband.

He made me this circle in the woods that exists for breathing beyond the words among us. I asked him to situate it near the creek, then took a nap. He got the location slightly off. His choice was better: mine would have been obliterated by the floods that year we married. Rains we barely noticed in our joy took out roads. This simply added to the excitement, as my first chore boots were an initiation to soaked leaf-floor and a perfect match to his.

Lorene, can you hear me? Why are you holding onto him? Isn't the next world a never-ending classroom that far exceeds the possible lessons of this circle, in these acres? What does his grief and his distance from me do for you now? Would you please let go? For his sake? For mine? I know you liked me. I know you were relieved, you understood *us.*

Lorene, I don't want your life. I don't want to waste words that never speak true. I know: Pops he is not. But have you ever watched someone tethered to reality lose it for the lost mom? Did your mother lose reality, when her laughing man's heart suddenly stopped? Pops's mother didn't know how to dress herself the day after he, the drunk, died because he'd picked out her clothes every morning. You had to initiate her to the chest of drawers, the closet—you handed her the permission with her bra and slip.

My generation, we had it worse, I hear you say—women were confined, men guarded bullishly. But do you understand the gravity, Lorene? I have nowhere to go. All bridges for backtracking went out in a heightened blaze. I signed up for—at the very last minute—the church of motherhood with its tremulous obligations. I took vows; I strapped myself to the mast. The new and the innocent are rife with need. I can't do this alone.

I give you these words from the stones of the creek. I followed it close to the property line, that foolish wire strung as if anyone ever stomped the other side. They don't; not this far back, where no one sees me, no others will be seen. The neighbors are stick figures with two fat bloodhounds who traverse the county road only to scare our geese. We don't talk; we wave from behind windshields. I don't talk to anyone but your son, Lorene.

Can you whisper to him at night? Tell him to get back on board? Am I selfish? You bet. But witness this haven of beauty, my mystery school. And hear these words that cost me so much breath given the climb he and I both made. You are not just "mother-in-law." You hold the key.

I am petitioning a dead woman among fallen trunks that couldn't take the incline. They gave up the ghost, but can you, Lorene? No one knows about this little talk. If I err, if I am crazed or sacrilegious, the woods keep secrets under rooted wrap, and I trust them for that.

I remain, barely your daughter-in-law and ever the understudy, awaiting your reply.

Book Two

11

Seven years later, at the roadside edge of some property sits a house where a couple try to have sex whenever their children sleep into the weekend. They are older parents and the teenage girls they shepherd without a clue are not the norm either. They have all lived here well over a decade, backed up by acres that grow their woods tighter, taller, that rampant twining the one constancy allowed. But still, these woods only turn down the volume of my fears, wipe the slate of chronic human tussles clean for a while, build me up for the next slice of chaos in BPD-land while waiting for something to break the impasse of the unsaid, waiting until I could bloom and persuade, incite and deliver. Oh really? The body had other plans.

Sierra at fifteen is broken by the rancor in the house. She hides behind the acquisition of report card As and a daily background of iPod love songs. Boyfriends? Watching the affections of classmate dyads trading saliva in the halls, she sneers, "Get a room!"

Nina, we assume is asexual, still autistic and prevented the subtleties of speech. We will never know how the changes that made her body voluptuous have re-made her thoughts. Asked if she likes boys, she answers with an emphatic, "Okay!" If there is a particular classmate she pines for at the one-on-one, behavioral therapy school, for once everybody keeps a pickax out of her privacy.

Deer populate wildly on the family property, symbols to the mother of the house of all she aspires to: clan camaraderie, hours available for the art of roaming, beauty and gentleness in a world ringed with ulterior motives. The father rows his tired boat to work in the small district courts of the region and travels on jets for administrative hearings where he becomes the hero of the hour, or a loser forever scourged.

Our long simmering batch of travail—that goes without explication—is allowed to ferment, while all within may suffer dark wishes for words to speak true, silently longing for the house to be filled with spume that could wreak the act of implosion.

≈

"Once you turned fifty," Asa remarked, "you were never the same."

"I guess so! It seemed like a final chance to find out who I really am."

Asa shook his head. "I never thought you'd go in for that crap."

"What crap might that be?"

"Finding yourself. So holy fucking trite."

He would never say, *I know you think you've lost something. I agree, you're not the one I married. She was so brazen. Such presence. Even power.*

And where did I go? I would never respond. *Into your movie. Your expectations. Your OCD regimens, your BPD surprises, knocking myself out to please. It's not what you wanted, was it? Then why did you lobby for it?*

Instead, I would couch my quest deep into the nobility of the land.

"What do you think I do down at the circle? Sleep? Pick my nose?"

"I think you're down there fuming at me."

"I'm down there trying not to!"

Asa expelled a breath. "It's always about you, isn't it?"

The land spreads away from the foot of the marital bed. Sixty acres that anchor trunks of oak and hickory, host a moody creek, allow spots of native prairie overrun increasingly by cedar. Does this jumble of topography love me back? I can't translate its silence, so love may indeed be buried in its song and the sigh of its partner, death. It delivers a welcome I count on, my path away from the hard world, whether the season shouts green or chooses stasis under snow. The land and I are present for each other.

The fantasy-man in his hairy pants must have taken his sex organs to a new locale, and I let him go. He held the mirror for the midlife marriage inside the nature-wrapped bedroom; he was the future of love that could have ignited the mystic's curriculum in an outdoor classroom. But what is wrong with Asa infects me too, a malaise I try to cloak whenever a daughter comes near. We all have each other in this family, and in many ways each of us has no one at all. In the woods I do not see this type of cross-abandonment and suspect the wind is but one channel that talks about what really matters.

Wildlife moves utterly concealed except for glimpses of the unhurried, white-tipped deer that circle the house and keep watch. Have they forgotten our archaic bond? Deer define my walkways through the wild. Neighbors call them a nuisance but sighting deer on the move is seeing the soul of the land set to ballet. Raccoons provide comic relief when they creep to the porch for scraps, and small bobcats a flash of fancy footwork, raiding our chickens. The deer have no less an appetite but like some women I have known, one never sees them eat.

Odocoileus virginianus: these whitetails leap and stand, a vision of all things God. They have no words, only loveliness to share. I wonder about the mind of a deer the way people ask their unseen deities: *do you hear me? Do you care for me?*

Dearest ruminant, do you understand how I protected you, turned away deer hunters, posted warning signs to predatory humans to *keep out,* followed your trails with faith that I am lauded for these works? I pretend that the deer garner my intentions with a placid nod, barely perceptible. It is tempting to attribute a connection when they raise their head at my appearance and stare as if wanting to talk in the old way, when humans could understand.

Deeply nocturnal, deer nose into the once glorious garden, turning away from the lost rows of burrs and plantain. They will amble to the back edge of the land, where cedars tower bare and hairy, reeking of ungulate flesh, for the deer often doze in groups. To step inside this realm is to think of Goodall with her gorillas, the young man living among grizzlies, Romulus and Remus raised by wolves. When I visit the deer's cedar haven, I am reaching for a common language. But there is nothing there that sees me. The acrid peace turns my steps away. Steps that quicken to seek the house, clinging to the hope that the real marriage still lives within.

12

In the still pause that Sunday morning bestows in exchange for the grueling week, what we as parents won't admit is that we traded midlife sex for the words among us—and now the parts that could have allied us refuse to work.

Elder sex is dry sex, or soft sex when needs cry out for the hard. My vagina fools me with its open portal, a slick entrance ready for anything. Part way up the passage it closes shop, although helpful creams and lotions grace the nightstand. It cannot be, as the crude parlance proclaims, that I have grown shut. I don't accept that a former busy thoroughfare simply caved in. Yet there is no detour. A man must put it in reverse and leave.

My husband, another resident of the over-fifty brigade, explains his flaccid penis with a new, situation-based mumble each time. I'm amazed at the creativity that stokes evasion, his agile leap into the space where little blames are always at hand, pinned to my errant words or motives. I have worn these sticky-notes of reprimand with the appropriate shame, raised to detract attention from the penis that doesn't work, learned to say it doesn't matter. Because it doesn't.

But truth does.

One time we ordered the erection-hoisting drugs, getting with the age-appropriate program. Visions of sexy older males on television commercials danced in my head as we prayed for a rising of soft tissue into turgidity. But only a fleeting note swelled from below, quickly extinguished by the pressure of expectations. Is it mind or matter that sets the trap? Or is it marriage?

We accept our lot and cuddle, for brief moments dodging the byways of criticism that history installs between us, as if the march of decades' passing have every right to sabotage the most natural act in the world.

As if there wasn't a darker event of the body and brain waiting to happen.

As if it would never come, nor would it explain all that was ever to unfold after that. It would come in November, worst month for cold, flu, holiday stress, and the mourning of autumn's demise into the gathering drums of barren cold. I thought lightning never struck the same place twice, so I didn't believe the big event was coming for us. I thought people learn from the mistakes of their ancestors, but I would turn out to be wrong.

But even before the last straw we were frigid elders. At least we didn't marry in winter but pointedly in the season of spring. Two days after April Fools' Day. Why do fools fall in love?

Why did the skies try to drown our love? It rained hard and non-stop the day we tied the knot. Was it an omen, the rain? When I took the land and Asa "to my hand, my heart and my spirit"—as our wedding vows proclaimed—I supposed that aging would bring out the beauty, the peace, and a certain congratulatory appeal about living in the country. I had vague thoughts about my advantage to become wizened and serene. I brushed over the part about hormones vacating en masse, leaving behind a foreigner I struggled to like.

A woman welcomes the word 'perimenopausal' on two counts when the sex drive falters. Finally, a name for the oops-stain and ping-pong mood while still hosting the monthly bleed. You are way past knowing the ropes of concealment and cramp management, so surprise leaks and odd schedules vex. Yet you harbor a gratitude that you're not yet menopause proper, a dread so stolid the word itself hurts. Later, you'll come to wish you'd gone straight to it without loitering in the confusing and chaotic peri-fog.

What a divide between the still-bleeding who hobnob at the river of fertility and the residents of the *Pause* rejoicing at unique gifts when the change pulls you in. This split will never be healed. Not in a world that salivates only for the nubile nude or breasty mama. Crones are an insult for living on past their juiciness.

But wait, say the self-help books—you can have totally awesome sex after sixty. It may be true, but it isn't easy and the more pressing question: is it natural? Were we supposed to live this long? No, but who's complaining?

Trekking headlong into the country of menopause—say one chooses not to try pharmaceuticals or potions—the place is like the Wild West. Lawless yet free, the past ever so superfluous. How will you feel about a preference for little sex and little memory of sex? You believe this state of mind to be permanent.

In the neighboring kingdom of andropause, similar conditions prevail. Citizens of both provinces know the sandpaper scrape of the vagina if provoked to make contact, the recalcitrance of the squishy male stump although pulled and practically flogged to death. When the pituitary gland cashes it in and the final trickle of hormones fades from ovaries and testicles, the brain reviles those hidden chemical dervishes with their years of driving pastimes. Sex is a bore. It means nothing. Let the young waste their time.

Meanwhile in Nature all manner of entities age, dry, wither and die. Instead, we make a religion of longevity. This is progress, I hear.

Parsing the enjoyment of sexual activity along with retirement and hobbies—in the cocoon of andropause or menopause, we need help to care. Sex hormones take vividness with them when they check out, but advertising renews the urge. Must aging sex become as requisite for seniors as hoisting a nine-iron with a sweet spot? Were Asa and I even seniors yet? Or simply pilgrims into a massive reordering of priorities, courtesy of some endocrine antics that had a testy way with emotion and thought?

Will the baby-boomer appetite for reforming attitudes allow the discard of the elder as a pitiful, pointless person? Putting my dry, lined hands into a stand of butterfly weed at the circle, I asked what indigenous population enacts such a heave-ho of elders or palliates their old with ersatz youth. In the vanishing worlds of tribal sanctity, the frailty of the last season is honored by others as carefully as the vulnerability of childhood. To regard numinous the tail end of the ride enhances community. Not to do so is like holding a basket with the bottom ripped out. Wisdom and spirituality slip through while busy achievers sail on, oblivious to what they dropped. The old sense their treasure but, tossed aside, they are quick to resent the pile-up of years as much as the next fearful heart. Hence the grumpy old man, the bitter old biddy.

I couldn't flag the day that neither furling mayapple nor scent of the rut didn't call my erogenous zones to attention. It was as if the land erotic went on hold—not crowded out by miscarriages and adoption and children growing in perplexity—but dropping its all into a vacancy that was me, still hanging on, theoretically, for I knew the land's power, and I missed my outdoor classroom. But I no longer wished to see a sensuous satyr along the creek. I would have yawned at his priapic display had he turned to me once more.

Orgasm was a chore indoors and outside; novel new thoughts swirled.

As did the lament: *what is happening to Asa?* Day by noticeable day he weakened and withdrew further. There were few words of any category among us. Was andropause alone to blame, or unmet grief, or a borderline running out of gas? I needed to settle on a label to explain my isolation.

To articulate a male body's march through andropause challenges the usual concessions to the aging process. How to get inside the fears about change that even the most secure couple can be subject to? Why for a woman is the chronic softness of penis during an amorous interlude an affront of such magnitude? Even when I could take it or leave it? Menopause urged me past the bedroom, habit compelled me to stay.

I couldn't correlate Asa's troubles with what I went through when my vagina shut down. In popular culture, speak-out about menopause was all the rage—there was even a musical! Andropause was not yet a topic for current events. I wasn't even sure that's what he "had." What if it was another borderline trick?

In the 1950s I grew up watching women immolate themselves in sundry prescribed ways. Even in the liberated Sixties one didn't question the sexual perfection of the male: *we* were frigid if they had a problem. As the television markets boner pills, what is my reaction after falling for it once? Embarrassment for the male sex while the drug companies air men's shame to capitalize on it, recasting limpness as a common glitch, easily tackled.

I can't think of anything less sexy than "chemical messengers" who run around tissues and organs igniting desire or withholding it. Hormones do other things too, but can you see one? Not without an electron microscope. Can you appreciate their dance? It's as simple as penis gathered in by vagina.

Hormones travel the body seeking their specific receptor sites: target cells broadcast *we're ready!* while hoarding those sites. The willing messenger needs a welcoming enclosure to proceed with such complex magic. It's not so much about a driver seeking a docking port as—here comes the tech word—*binding*. Hormones *bind* to their receptor sites. Binding, bonding.

The scientific language turns evocative: once a hormone meets its receiving buddy, a "cascade of reactions" ensues toward a "burst of synthesis." Mmmm. Intense.

Erectile dysfunction becomes an acceptable if not profitable malady because the times will repair any stigma they care to. In my youth there was no such free pass because limp ones were seldom heard of. Shushed pity covered the rarity. I had one friend who dated a man who couldn't get it up for her even though he longed to do so. To a one, her friends found it terribly sad and purely, indelibly, his psychological deficit.

Asa was once Mr. Easy Riser, standing up to the occasion, staying the course well and wittingly then coming with a normal aplomb. Andropause, he passed off with a shrug. Each failed attempt to interest the deflated member was attributed to a source of distraction, and many he had to do quite a creative reach for. Mostly, it was my fault. He was afraid he was hurting me, given the menopause dryness and all.

I kept doing what I'd always done: going to the wild as time allowed. Tossed between the eroding cliffs of estrogen and progesterone, I shifted, and the land didn't intrude. I needed to be hailed, not held. Hailed by silence, and the absence of the artificial. Grateful for the chamber, however deserted and dry, where self meets age for the next course of study.

Asa and I stumbled on through the *Pauses* hoping there was an alternate route—affection—that would hold the marriage together. We glossed over the lack of hot sex as many couples do and listened to favorite love songs that reminded us that those twenty years in the orbit of each other were worth quite a lot.

Pause Me

Dear changing body that missed out on childbirth (relieved to have bypassed that ravage), now careening into the badlands of menopause: I want to be friends. Familiar with how I dread you, I suspect you won't listen to me. Mistrust fills the spaces between us as we come to this last reckoning—the useless womb, crone's season—before we part at death. I long to reconcile, for there is already enough suspicion to go around, but yes, body, sometimes I hate you.

The land symbiotic neutralizes this toxic dance. Could this be the real reason I return? My body is something else out there in the land, nothing faked or forgotten once it is hailed or held.

Yet aches and irritations fill me. Body, you ladle me sorrow, you make me want to be alone to think. How nice to forsake tampons and the bitch-phase of the month, but what is this? Roller coasters of the mind that slash at the heart, leave metal in my mouth and spark at my heel. I need room for all this activity. The land keeps gushing fertilely, then dying to winter nubs, without reflection or posturing. The land sticks to Simple. *Come in,* states the circle's embrace, *and be yourself, whatever that is.*

Prayer is so elusive in the eye of this storm, and I'm no ascetic who transmutes pain to gold. But let me try a skosh of humility, to craft a devotional that may bolster me one more day:

May I abide the night sweats that erase a place on the sheets to sleep.

May I look at my face in the mirror, beholding a stranger, and hold the gaze.

May I slow before the plates of food that tempt me to engorgement.

May I learn when to conquer: the stiffness of joints, the hands turned to claws because who cares to moisturize?

May I learn acceptance: the hair once so voluminous that produces gobs detached in the bath.

May I ride the puffs of fog and fatigue that promise a way out: where are you, wisdom?

May I weather the scorn of people who look askance at "old." People who give me the senior discount right away, who reach out to help me duck under the fence lest I land butt first in the dirt.

May I find something else to set the clock of my moods by. The cycle of woman's blood accruing to no end has worn out like a broken toy, battery discontinued.

I'm released into vast time with no excuse.

13

You only get one menopause. Replete with loss of libido—I had none, so the land became a temple for something else besides my body hot for beauty. It became a necessary, vibrant container for me and Thought Woman as I imagined her.

In Hopi and Navajo narratives, she is both grandmother and industrious spider, weaving the world into place. The skein of thread is her thoughts, free to create the infinite variety of landscape and creatures, the ideas of how matter can wear and tear, how humans fit, even the nature of storms. I was obsessively tuned into my thoughts these days. My mind was an echo-chamber of spinning wheels, and oh, the aloneness.

But what freedom that was! Released from the need to please and endlessly weigh the relationship's balances, I started to look forward to Asa's next trip to the airport.

In marriage, Whodunit First can become a favorite game. Did I check out so completely in menopause because Asa was emotionally absent—hiding away in his anxious layers (shed only with television or marijuana), working like a fiend through an increasing number of hours per day? Did the hazardous words among us when I was in my prime pollute what time we had?

Or did menopause trigger andropause—beyond words, beyond the barrage called stress? I'm talking about a pheromone-studded, sync-up that burgeons from married proximity—akin to how female roommates cycle on the same menstrual-clock together. Thinking myself indisposed in the grip of meno-strangeness, I may have been subliminally inviting Asa to grow old along with me.

But by the time we were both pausing, the inability to hold the reality of the other's heart was severely compromised. Contempt was an easy out that enabled Asa, but for once I wasn't the only target. His work started to plague him as petty and routine, yet he doubled down on clinging to the attorney-persona, having little else. Meanwhile the daughters made it impossible to split up—we were too old to be that unwise. But lines were drawn, and my quest was the same as ever: to provide myself with the healing needed by following the directives of wordless Nature. Trying to decide whether my motivations were self-centered, or if self-care was a dead end. I could see the shine in the eyes of those who had reached a safe port, hinting that menopause was a perfect storm not to be missed.

It's a secret we're not told, the classic case of the woman surprisingly freed: *peri*menopause was the worst, not this dry plain upon which one could see for miles. I looked outward at the world and wanted what I'd missed all those years as a midlife mom isolated in rural containment, imagining satyrs and sharing pillow talk with trees. I looked inward most of the time where others' voices were an intrusion. The constancy of the land with its changing four seasons erased the tags Asa and I wore—Pause persons, the Border-line and the Bewildered, career and possessions the paltry hooks to hang our battered hats on.

≈

Sometimes the land I loved seemed a repository of empty dreams. The Lake's overlook was a popular spot with accessible grandeur, but more often I picked a trail winding through a local conservation district. It held a murky lagoon that was breathtaking with a sense of fetid-creepy and darkly magical.

Water barely touched its hem to this and other inlets that couldn't be reached by car and were too shallow for boats. Over a vast field of healthy forbs and prairie grasses, the moon rose with grand drama. Climb a small hill and see sweet coves on all sides thick with waterfowl a blessed distance from jet-skis and pontoons. The quiet was roomy and personal, far from the Lake tourist point where the pinking of sunsets was widely attended.

Woods were not the place's strong point, although swampy willows lined the trail until hikers had to veer along a generous farmland creek, banked with outcroppings as big as twin beds side by side. Leave the concrete path and wonder if you're still on tax-payers' land—the creek paired its stone-draped shallows with pits of depth, logs thrown across like high wire for the daring. I wished for that kind of balance but found it was not a side effect of the Pause.

Once again, I was cheating on my land. A novel face and body—I was hardly immune to that, these eyes of change seeing differently. There were other gifts: someone else protected and tended these grounds, and those people were rarely around. The place sat in the poor county, not a favorite of the spandex and bike helmet crowd. Many features of its sprawl matched eddies and shortcuts in my mind. I happily availed myself of stolid picnic tables for cracking open a journal to unload.

The Pause left me with lots to say. Intimacy at this spot was palpable but not physical: like talking your heart out when you are talking with one who only has ears for you. And who's going to poke around in a swampy nub of a lake that floods and recedes? I often chose the bench there just for the stark scene: ghostly dead trees worn gray, at first sight a meditation on death, but in reality a sturdy suburb for the birds and a necessary culling for diversity of the arboreous stand as a whole. It was clear that walkers and bikers avoided the niche.

These days were my first-ever vacation from the primacy of sex on the brain. There was room for so much more! Before the Pause, my marriage to the land was an extension of, or respite from, my vows to Asa. Did libido really cease-fire? Or did it slip away to another realm, becoming a keener sense than the urge to merge?

When hormones take their retirement, paranoia may flare—there's no escaping that. Suffering can be a daily chore. But what was it like long ago, before aging became the dreaded unspeakable? Did the social group applaud because change in the life cycle was gods-given, a change so sweeping it was viewed a divine event? Was a preoccupation with the self, post-dominion of the cycle of ovulation and bleed, such a crime? Or a once-in-a-lifetime, on-site vigil at the gates of the sacred?

Menopause was the moment I stopped crying. Crying over my marriage, crying for my children's every hurt, crying over lost babies, crying because I let go my career to attend to a special-needs child, crying for my stasis as a woman who'd rather isolate than elbow through the crowd. Tears may have gone due to the overall drying tendency at work in the body, but that was fine. There had been so many. They had worn out their welcome.

I didn't waste much time taking myself to task for hiding out in order to simply be, because I didn't feel like a runaway. I felt at home in lonesome places like these, designed for hikers who weren't here. Yet it was getting harder to return to the car, to drive back to the acres Asa gave up on, with the girls caught in the middle of it all. Menopause was handily available to blame, although the refrain kept ringing as I studied the Borderline playbook:

It was time—not to run like hell—but to change the rules of the game.

Cry Quietly, Mama

As the dinner assembles from pans and oven and chopping board, birds take to the topmost branches. They alight where the sun is golden-on-green.

When the children trail toward bed by way of bath, woods that watch the proceedings relax and respire, ready to droop too, slowly dropping carbon into the yard and between the flanks of creeks whose waters cool slightly.

While the husband keeps his tender scars covered and rails at how every person he encounters thuds stupidly into trouble, the deer leave their bedding to part the curtains of dusk, fooling predators for the ecstasy of supping on fungi and night-buds.

When the giver gives all away and hides behind a locked door, sly moles dome up the soil just beyond walls wherein Mama lies on her side and weeps for the very last time.

When the husband takes his last toke to erase both demons and bureaucracy, then sleeps miles away in the same bed as his wife, stars fall at random toward the hills. Cool updrafts are rebuffed by two-storied shelters full of belongings.

When the next day of obligations arises, the panting of flowers in thick bushes broadcasts seminal mysteries for short moments that wrap the dawn.

Like clockwork, we disregard these spirits. Gratitude to them, for still they attend us.

How we humans huff and puff inside our little cages and sometimes come forth to rend landscapes with diggers and mowers as if to beat back what could have been—forgive these violations for they constitute rape under the guise of religion.

Greenness, in all ways great, teach us right passion for you once more, passion that throttles the susceptible, knee-bends the haughty, sends the love-addicted woman back to the See-All. Let leaves and field mice crack the cellulose siding and enter, as Mama, no longer indentured, revivifies in night-dreams the half-hidden and wild.

14

I never bled in synchrony with my daughters, never shared the cycle of the shedding womb, meno-removed and free from that bleed. But what did I miss?

In on their first bra buying, the explanations of period pads and mood swings, and questions about sex from the youngest. "The talk" was abridged with the daughter unable to formulate such questions, who tended to openly sit astride a stuffed animal rubbing privates with morbid concentration. Nina and I spoke of "woman's blood" to come, and I drew the usual conclusion: autism doesn't care a whit about something it has no sensory experience with, or no definitive picture for a tag.

I was a guide faking it. To Sierra, I spoke with an earnestness that hid amusement because it was so hard to recall when any of it mattered. As the two girls turned to womanhood, I was slipping into something else, doing my best to provide resources and support, but I was no comrade. I also had gratitude because neither one of them was crazy for boys in a world where boys could change them forever.

It was so safe yet surreal to see my girls turning into adults, for my identity as Older Parent—and the impact of raising them at midlife with Asa—seemed to eclipse their ascent into adolescence. Would a younger mom experience a vague, tense rivalry, awkward scenes surfacing from her own pubescent past, whether lurid or a line toed well? Luckily, I viewed the growing of daughters into women as a wonder to behold, curios along the parental trail, the spotlight on change and no boys allowed. Handy that it went so well.

It meant I was spared the very worst thing, a gashing open of memories about how berserk I went even before my first bleed, dreaming of The One. I'd learned well that boys were the apex of what was deemed attainable in life, better than girls. Girls were only for pedestals and projections. In classrooms I stared at the latest crush endlessly, dying to be noticed. I became a hippie for permission to be blatant and "forward." I couldn't wait to be asked and risk waiting too long, which was any time two seconds past the moment I fell in love from afar.

The donning of love-beads and leather headbands wasn't a moment to push Nature out of my way. Embedded in the music, hair, and clothes was the tacit understanding that we, the freaks of Nature, knew Nature better than the others. It's been said that the counterculture bloomed into color the way that Nature does, that we were promiscuous as She, that we were animals on the loose.

I stole away in full hippie-regalia to the river behind the college where my dad worked, to write poetry on the banks held by cottonwoods. But mostly, I bore down on finding myself through sex. Counterculture showed the way, but females were still only a walking set of genitals to screw, nail, ball, get a piece of, fuck. To contemplate any of that during the Pause, I met with alternating guffaw and indignation, with deeper tones of wistful-sad for the girl who I was.

Luckily, no daughter had interest in my past; in fact, Sierra didn't want to know. Nina lived totally in the present and accepted me for all she could not see.

But there are currents that infect a family, inside a house holding scents and daydreams season after season, and these girls turning pubescent made their elder mother long for more. Made me long for Asa, that he would be my boyfriend again, but the words among us were firm: *none of that.* Maybe my breathlessness out in the woods was puberty redux—a developmental stage that would lift me after initiation into an even higher sexual fervor. I could feel the promise, even with hormones on the run. The return of the land erotic as never before?

What seems universal in good sex is that you lose your body through the body of the other. When the woods swallowed me whole, I no longer had sagging jowls or a sore back that clipped my walk. When the creek said *come here*, I was liquid when we touched. Not a bone in my body asserted itself, and my mind dissolved all memory but the sensation of water on skin. There were no eyes anywhere, thankfully: the seeing was tactile and the lust to lust came and went.

I rode a parallel track to the girls turning, harboring my own revolution, but how to tell them? It never occurred to me. Secretive as a new teen, I rolled in my bed of this nature-place or that one, genitally chaste but mind on fire, alone but unashamed of a body galumphing through change.

≈

"What is it now?"

"The new caregiver can't come out here and the meltdowns have been fierce all day long." My anger was building.

Asa's shoulders drooped another centimeter. "Is it the end of the world?" He meant, *be strong, I'm at the end of my rope, too!*

"I'm beat, I'm nearly sick, I need a break."

"Yep, your life is so much worse than anyone else's."

I wheeled around like I always do, grabbing the bait because I must: "If you were only here more! To help me!"

Asa opened a kitchen cabinet. "What do you want for dinner?"

He lunges, then wipes his spear as if it had simply nicked me. And I fall in line, depleted. Big martyring sigh. "I don't care. I'll eat it if you make it."

"Yet I never give you any help."

"Don't torture me for showing how I feel!" I had lost, why bother?

"Don't state what's not true." He was calm now. A point scored. Or he'd crushed another sliver of his soul as happens so freely in the Borderline wars.

"Why is it 'helping' when you're just doing your share of the work?" I tried for the last word, but Asa pressed his lips together and rolled up his sleeves. Recalling the fan on high in the guest room when we slept at his parent's house, I had to hand it to him: he refused to engage like they had, trading bitterness for bitterness until the night bled. He called it quits on his own time, of course, when stamina flagged. That benefitted us both.

I leaned on the land more than ever the days when my husband was rarely home. He flew three times a week across the country to represent strangers at hearings before administrative judges. Asa's travel gave us respite from the Four Horsemen. I could sometimes access the man I married when his suitcase rolled in the door. My job was in his office: billing and filing and answering the phone. My other job was trying to keep the disabled kid's needs on track while arranging for her sibling a semblance of normalcy. That dream took shape via my fuzzy interpretations of other families' lives.

I continued to puzzle over the impact of Asa's mother's death. I worried he'd been her surrogate spouse, her pride and joy carried to extremes. It served them both, for his father was a rapid-cycling "rage-aholic," said Asa in a rare use of psychobabble. His youth centered on dodging the man's presence. Mother and son united under their ruler. As the two who possessed more education and civility but no power, they could only bide their time. Asa found a way out with college and a white collar, Lorene through illness and early death.

I realize it's a serious charge I'm leveling at his mom: making son a surrogate-spouse. Emotional incest. How could I know for sure? It helped me make sense of a closed system the two of them seemed to be, as I turned to the land for attention. Their bond that once seemed so woman-affirming ended up pitting her, in death, against me. Still, I couldn't entirely villainize his mother for cleaving to Asa, and in time dropped the worry that she crossed the line.

There was no evidence that she wove a toxic bond. She carefully prepared and encouraged him for an escape from their small town and the surly male parent. Had she launched teary-eyed ploys to keep him by her side, Asa would have rebelled. I had to admit that despite her inertia and disappointments, his mother strove to lend a guiding hand, even if she couldn't forestall her own demise.

Women weren't forthcoming in those self-effacing days. Asa said she used to lose herself in books, she cooked and cleaned sporadically, and she did avail herself of the one social outlet available: church. Only her smoking, diabetes, and ultimate undoing by a stroke telegraphed her dismay. Relishing the corny phrase because he believed it, Asa often said, "my mother was a saint."

I knew Lorene's memory still meant more to him than I did. Unresolved grief was the director of his days, and I was a stand-in allowed on stage. I grieved Odysseus's stay on random islands and his focus on the mythical women there who held sway—it's stretching the analogy, but his mother had her Circe sense of command, her Siren song, and her jealous but ultimately fair Calypso side.

I still thought of Penelope, trying to keep the home together while things edged further out of control. But like Odysseus's queen, I believed in the man's return. It's a matter of dispute whether Penelope was faithful to her mate during his long absence. No doubt about it, I cheated when I went into the woods and put all thoughts of my human spouse aside. I still thought about the oak-eyed manspirit, and I could feel him, sometimes, watching me. But the detritus of cultural bias spun a hole and I fell in: *he wouldn't want me anyway, I'm old and dried up.*

Stepping into the circle or sitting by the creek, I could count on a change of heart, deepening minute by minute, or if I was rewarded with significant time, hours by the creek could uncoil my hurts and catapult my senses with the beauty. Fierce mindfulness on my part unknotted tension and revealed that I was in a different world now. I felt heard and asked myself how this could be. Menopause gave the surroundings a different quality—austere, temple-quiet, but no less electrically charged. Was this just another side of the land erotic? Was hot-to-trot the only way to get a buzz, or could The Great Pause be a graduate-level course in how to see past the veil of the ordinary?

The more I valued this time that started to look like anything but a pause, I literally took problems to the woods or Up Top, and worked them out with clouds, animal sightings, water loping by—voicing ragged and let-'er-rip prayers. Such actions were risky to confess to the secular clergy of therapy, the ultimate arbiters of who fits in and who is unhinged. Cleaving to the People World is how you please them if you follow the rules: you don't personify the outdoors to the extent of a torrid attachment.

But both science and mysticism assert it's a cosmic error to hold notions of separate or stationary molecules. My molecules laced into the big rock in the creek, its immovable, ultra-hardness merely energy vibrating much slower than my mobile flesh and bone. Rock didn't have the ability to jump and run like me, nor perhaps pity itself for its limitations—but then I would never know how to surrender to squirrels shredding hedge-apples on my head.

Maybe my sitting rock pitied me for tagging it with concepts like being "slow" energetically. The trance I was in wasn't a dangerous loss of "boundaries," but a deliberate snub of the edict to stay in my own skin with my limited story of how rocks never daydreamed, and my thoughts alone create the world.

What about mind then? Wasn't it a separate container, privately owned? It sure felt like it, full of pressing judgments about Asa and the kids and all my failures and future schemes. But what of its changing maneuvers? Tripping over itself, reacting to everything it takes in? How can I walk five minutes to a thirty-foot circle in the woods with a few rocks placed at every quadrant and in minutes forget the humans who bedevil me?

Because sensuality with nature, even from inside the bodyless, mind-bending hormone-leaving consciousness of age, carries the longing for human contact into the "I" that I experience as dissolved by the touch of all that is.

15

B ut of course, I fell back into this pique: why can't I figure
out my life? I wondered if I burrowed soul-first into the
land to anthropomorphize a replacement for truly living.
This type of thought train loved to take the menopausal mind for a
ride.

Anthropomorphize. A big word strapped with reprimand,
implying that we blithely remake the land and its wild things in our
image, complete with human parts and motivations. Self-lauding
and self-absorbed, we translate every feature of nature to look,
sound or act like a bipedal primate known for its language and
tools. Why is that a terrible thing?

The argument goes: *get out of your species and cultivate wordless
awe! You say a platypus reminds you of Uncle Fred because you're afraid
of beholding a creature that confounds you.* A deeper worry is that

whatever we twist into our image is deemed free to use, and we'll eventually abuse this privilege.

I didn't worry about any of these misgivings unless I was in the house, my nose stuck in a book about how fast the planet was losing ground to human folly. Doubts about "the environment" faded fast under moonlight or clouds waiting to burst, because love was the only activism I could muster. I opened fully to what I got and doubted that a leaf or dragonfly disapproved if I saw them as friends. Maybe fellowship, if not family, has no boundaries once we stop asking human-only brethren to fill every void. My environmentalist books rightfully pleaded, scolded, and cajoled for better behavior toward the wild. But so rarely did they say a word about love for it all in the same way that flesh knows its own kind as kin.

The power of affirmation I drew from my land versus the disapproving air around a human marriage partner made me wonder. Is there a positive place for anthropomorphizing, could it be more than a comforting default? Why couldn't one be married to her own chosen piece of place, personified as bride and lover?

We most often rest our imaginations in authority figures: Mother Earth, Father Sky. I had family like that in the deeper woods: the imposing oak I regularly addressed as Grandfather, a group of walnuts on the north ridge I honored as the Three Mothers—each had whorls or indentations to their bark that made deep spaces like wombs. I went like a child to these often enough, as the need for parental support never fades. With menopause the Socratic Method replaced the soggy Kleenex as I tried to answer their questions and get them to answer mine.

Then the scent of the rut accidentally invades a willing center in the brain. A bird of prey draws a circle in the air on top of you, screes and looks down, and you are gazed upon. An imaginary Man O' The Woods finds a soft bed of leaves, reclines, and fondles his sex with an affectionate concentration. As age pushed me onward, these visceral treats were stored for later, whenever the night sweats ended.

The silence was my sedative, lit by birdsong and branches scraping, pinned by moments so languid I could barely get my body out from beneath it when the watch in my pocket called time.

If I Was Flora or Fauna or Fixed

If I was flora or fauna or fixed in place, says the human heart ripped to shame by ecocide—and I could bring with me this heart while I inhabit others—I'd project onto beings such anger-pity-ecstasy plus a humanly squired freedom to reflect on stupid human tricks. Before these creatures, anthropomorphizing is second to taking my licks.

If I was Bird I would sing for the sky, nest to a just-so circle, scrap nightly with my neighbors for the best sleeping limb, and snack like there was no tomorrow. Who cares how I embody Spirit for the big-legs, those softskin talkers filling the space down there—binoculars trained to see me glistening—the ones who, for all their obsessions with my feathers and song, can't control the urge after "birdwatching" to overlook their complicity in the paving of green vistas to amplify greenbacks they store in hip-bulging wallets?

If I was Fish in toxic brown river, I would breathe up concentrics from below the surface, flip over the dam with a gymnast's aplomb, tune to my school, and read the molecules for enemies who want me. How everyone hunts my flesh, quick to spit out fin or scale! Do I know I am a trove that yields luscious flakes with delicate ease? Am I a swimmer or a miracle carried along: *downstream* the vision that never materializes, CAPTURE the only drawback to my neatly natatory life? Meanwhile, I navigate human trash in heaps on my floor.

Even as a Firefly—or twelve, united by group mind in serial backyards, winking off and on in magical dissonance—I would continue to flick and signal: *look at me come love me.* I would let the viewers find me beautiful and agreeable, and even glide to the smooth prison of a Mason jar—but later, if released back to the vast meet and greet of winking lights, I would find my mate for the night and keep fit for the next one to come.

Thankfully, I am not the horse in small pen at the edge of town—a gelding filthy from its mud-lot, desultory at the alfalfa crib, with a thick droop of forelock that blocks the bicyclists and joggers clipping past. In this eternal drowse he chaws, his owner a dream who rarely comes. *How he used to pinch my belly with saddle and take me to the gateless hills to wander halter-only, sun-laced, browsing new forbs .. how we were one.*

16

The drought that drained the creek was over at last. I'd been suspicious: someone upstream was messing with me, damming or siphoning, or what? Scant rain pointed to the facts, but how could my sacred stream, my lifeline for clearing emotional debris, disappear for so long? When the sky opened and water returned to Buck Creek, it offered to put many things back the way they were.

I lowered my hands in the clarity of fresh wet. Humble pebbles were precious as pearls. I was loved again: the water was a fully satisfied snake throughout my land and onward. Order returned; nurture resurged. How to install it in the vicinity of the heart? How to share? I would tell my family, "The creek is running again!" and see if that didn't change their story.

When she was five, the youngest waded in with a bar of soap and washed herself head to toe. These days she is modest as a Victorian and sleeps with her phone. The eldest is at her bath for hours most nights, ruminating in silence, surrounded by squeaky toys she listlessly pokes. My terror regarding her lost joy is a scream I suppress daily.

But I gather the creek water to my extremities and rejoice. I know there will be tadpoles, striders, unpleasant bacteria, and Ag runoff to come, but this day, these few inches of transparent silk rub me right.

These are my legs submerged—water dresses them up, glossy. Tiny varicosities are starting to show at the knees, but water doesn't care. Today it's the gentlest massage therapist ever. But if my husband would even come to look, a big if, he wouldn't touch a drop.

Asa never learned to swim. I feel the deepest pain for his loss. He avoids even the shallow end of a pool. How do you live without water to enfold you? He says as a younger man he'd float on an air mattress at the reservoirs, tempting fate. I missed so much of his freer days.

But what a way with water's inhabitants, with all his paraphernalia on the banks known for bounty. When I tried to learn fishing, I irritated him. Too many questions about technique, too much talk. *Let me in, let me in*—I was at it again. I should have moved down the bank, watched, and tried to catch his state of mind. Meditation? Conquest? Could he admit it doesn't work with little kids along, even though he bought them their own Tweety Bird and Bugs Bunny poles?

I can't stop wondering what Asa really thinks about what I do at the creek or while roaming the land. When I'm away and at it, does he imagine me, or erase me? Does he think I am lucky, silly, privileged, energetic, repetitious, healing, daydreaming, or out there only fuming at him? Does it substitute for his own forays if he could but let himself go? Am I a piece of him out walking, dispensing a vicarious salve? Or does he not picture me at all—basking in a short vacation from his harried partner?

Why don't I ask him? Because if even one of the Four Horse-men rode in to answer, I would never forgive. That's the thing about the words among us: rarely do they care if they are true. Asa never blocks me in any way from finding the door, so I choose to hear this: *I know the land means a lot to you.* My treks are inviolate, and for this I am grateful and because of this I am alive. Our ragged way with words stops here.

≈

Midlife or menopause, exhaling at the creek was more real to me than those ties gerrymandered by clock, school, job. Mom-feel-goods were fewer as the girls matured; the challenge of steering a special-needs daughter was exhausting. I pictured cozy cabins on select sites in the woods where I couldn't be reached, returning to the main house less and less. Going feral. What's wrong with this fantasy? A drained mom should dream of spas and margaritas.

What about getting more serious about "land use?" Asa often said we needed to make these acres pay for themselves. Plant a more commercial orchard. Grow shitake mushrooms in the woods. Raise goats. Not that he possessed the energy. It would have been me, slogging it out alone, more domestic servitude while the wild tempted on either side, forbidden by deadlines to serve up solace or sensuality. I've considered the premise that hard labor, mindfully embraced, becomes its own reward, that the body's willful inten-tions to sculpt a homestead could manifest character as the day toils on. Not a bad idea. Simply not up to it.

Then what *am* I doing out here? It boils down to "listen up!" To overcoming the edict to seek advice from a therapist, for ther-apists guarantee they'll hack a way out of a messy mind. Where are the initials for a disorder I could toss about my shoulders as I fly out the door and head creekward? The land doesn't keep these items in stock.

Nor do you discuss an erotic obsession with your land casually among friends. Friends were a niche endeavor anyway—there were work friends, autism friends, parenting friends, cyber friends, and even spiritual friends but no Land Friends. A few had walked with me to my circle and beyond. None saw it as I did, all my sensors tuned for an empathetic note. What was I waiting for that would constitute the founding of a secret, earth-mystics club? Putting the specifics of my concerns to lichen and snowmelt, they often have something to say. Their point of view deviates from the human one.

If only I could give something of value to this place, something determined by the land and on the land's timetable. I wanted to be a good partner who doesn't ask for too much, keeps her appetites in check. I wanted to be a good woman who gives in exemplary fashion. So far, I'd been on the receiving end.

But protection proved evident in the deeds we could do. The No Hunting signs went up around the perimeter shortly after we moved in. Good ol' boys that came calling with coon dogs were rebuffed in the driveway, even by the "man of the house." I beamed at Asa for not backing down, even as an ex-hunter who once collected firearms. These were summarily sold when I freaked out about them.

When an emissary from the former owners visited, she wailed her clan's lament: "But you're not *doing anything* with the place!" It's true that erosion, cedars, and fallen deadwood were having their way with these acres. But native grasses surged Up Top where dryland farming once pulled at the soil without reprieve. Doing nothing: no logging, no mono-cropping or chemical assault? I felt good about it.

I also gave to these acres my praise and rapt attention—an effort to pave a two-way exchange. Knowledge of the landscape's body adding and deleting itself over time, memorized in detail and celebrated with high emotion. What if such acts of devotion improve all molecules, from soil to sky?

The deep-shaded environmentalist will assert that the land doesn't need humans for anything. Does it need milkweed or a nighthawk? Of course! But *we* are not worthy. What *we* have done is beyond selfish and mean.

I drew the line at spending what time I had outside gnashing my teeth against the land-rapists. My ardor blocked despair. Besides, anger was plentiful enough indoors. When a house founded on love becomes a house of rage, it's a daily chore to ride roughshod over an eruption. The words among us waxed once again, spilling from the chronic resentments we sought to suppress. But pressed silence collects in corners, sifts to the floor. I should have vacuumed and dusted daily—would that have helped? Or would the smaze of anger only rise to the attic, one measly door to block its way, its weight floating down the steps as we woke to another day?

If only people had come over, drinking beer, telling their stories, like the neighbors in the beginning. How did we isolate, until it had been too long to imagine anything else? How did the anger become routine—even with the antics of puffy kittens and odd strays populating the rooms, doing their best to spread cheer or demonstrate how to relax? Asa and I fell to old flinches re-worked into new paranoias. Show me this kind of anger in the land—never mind people construing storms as Nature being vicious. Is the Earth angry at what we've done to "Her?"

Cataclysms happen, and she will expel us. Or kill us. On the way we'll still howl over not getting what we want: more oil, more beach houses, more of us grabbing and extending and extolling our right to do It, the next big thing.

I decided not to pray for the Earth. She will unfold herself in drama or peace accordingly. I have decided people are the broken, the dangerous, the ones who should be prayed for.

I walk sixty acres back and forth to believe the world is vibrant with wonder and hope, not dead-end human frustrations igniting the worst potential future. It seems hypocritical though to bleed for humanity while harboring resentments in my house, sores that don't heal. I began to see the infection spread to the youngest, who cannot take any criticism, will not show her homework or art, and retreats at the barest whiff of adult "splaining." Isn't that what teenagers do? Or did we transplant fears she'll need decades to unravel?

I'd very much like to pray for homo sapiens, but I'm too tapped out to do it. If I pray for them, then who prays for me?

17

Autumn is sex magic for the eyes.

The leaves keep pace with change but it's the accents that grab you. We learn to label such things scenic, even gorgeous. We un-learn how they tease the libidinous heart.

Dots of swelled burgundy bring buckbrush out of obscurity. The rondure of hedge-apples, when foliage leaves the branch, reveal a tree-statue with numerous breasts like ancient Artemis of Ephesus. Tiny asters hide in spent grasses, their lavender eyes seeking mine. I look up: the smear of clouds is soft and close, a pillow for fresh sprites of air.

Then why does the season invoke sorrow?

Another little death on the wooded plains.

≈

I wasn't too shy to ask my silent partners: what do I do? I asked them all the time, too much perhaps. I queried rivers, talked to the moon on a regular basis, stepped into swirls of falling leaves to petition the breeze. Any feature of nature might harbor a helping sign. Animal didn't speak louder than mineral, and no flower was wiser than a changeable sky. I had a few special mentors on the land, conceived as private tutors because they rarely saw other humans. They determined the date and length of the session.

Sitting at the center of my cleared circle, facing east where the woods opened onto sunrise sliced by buzzards keeping an eye out, I could bitch and grouse, but these days I rarely named names: persons back at the house need not be evoked.

That was going to change without warning.

One morning a message intruded, not easy to digest. I went out for blessed blankness, beauty naturelle, and hearing what I wanted to hear. Instead, this dialogue came and engendered doubt, fidgeting and scowling, and an urge to complain when the land didn't thrill me.

What if the whole place was sick of me bowed or boiling over? Sick of the same old question, from the deepest, most exasperated part of myself: *why do I stay with Asa?* It was a riddle I traced from every angle. If he's so unavailable, disconnected, contemptuous, and ultimately a material guy, am I a glutton for punishment?

Enough about him, said the dew cloying my feet, *let's talk about you.*

When "your" acres afford the privacy to be truly alone with the land, you have the privilege of talking out loud to yourself, or to nothing, no one, or to anything that cared to pipe up. I understood my great fortune and privilege; I had them. Some Ones.

"I'm no victim," I said out loud. "What about his BPD?"

These voices I hear outdoors—from within, magnified by without—judgment and entrapment aren't their way. *What to do, what to do?* echoed a bouncy bush of wild rose as I stepped over some coyote scat on the trail, sporting a frenzy of flies. Plants leaned in, alert; I was gathering a crowd.

I knew my past strategy with the family was broken: the one where I resign myself to the negative, dark, disappointing events as inevitable, my lot. Then somehow the beauty and the silence wash it into a semblance of forgetfulness, like bandage and balm for yet another confrontation with them.

Cynicism is one way to get by, through dimming the world, and it is an inherited knack. If one sees the lack, the lesser, the grim "reality," the least-positive perspective—it slams the lid down on enthusiasm or hope. My elders chose to be urbane and critical, lest their joy be squashed. On this morning I needed a hefty shot of endorphins to ditch their habit of gloom.

At the circle, I kneeled to the center altar stone, clutching its sides, neck loose and head down. The limestone was cool to my rough palms, the ashen shadows of spent lichens dotted the rim like buttons. If only this was as simple as pushing for a new outlook or idea. I was at the end of some line. But the land was tired of messing with me.

Get up, the circle itself urged, *walk creekside. So what if in your first family you learned to protect yourself by being grumpy and acting superior, combative and on guard—there's more than one way to grow up, and you can do it now.*

At water's edge, little stones complemented the low burbling, no two alike. I scanned up the hill rising steeply ahead, where once a desired fantasy-man climbed away. He was, and is, the land erotic. This time I felt told to pick as many pebbles as I could, each one to represent something about Asa that was precious. One at a time, slowly, with feeling.

I thought of Asa reminding me before he left for court this morning how we would be buying fireworks for the Fourth of July. For once I didn't complain about the expense. The man was crazy for them and wouldn't be restrained by budget anyway. Usually I griped: *what a waste of cash!*

But for some reason I held my tongue. Because, in fact, watching Asa filling his basket with rockets and spark-emitters, high-flyers and booming gunpowder—easily including the daughter who shares his excitement—I feel good, if I'll let me. The man is all about holidays and taught me how to savor them after years of jaded resignation to their cyclic inconvenience.

At Yuletide, the faded tree ornaments he had as a child mingle with our growing cache each year, while odd music plays for weeks ahead of time. (All my life I will have to hear "Christmas in Prison" by John Prine, or it won't be the holidays.) The attention to details of the Thanksgiving meal is an administrative feat he relishes, especially after he married a former vegetarian who never learned how to cook meat. Asa solemnly decorates and hides eggs, not with that stand-aside, parental air—and not like a gleeful kid either—but because it's Easter. On his birthday and Father's Day, he expects to be treated like a king.

None of this began with the advent of children: it was there before and through the start-up of us. The honor given to special days and their special rituals warms me through and through. "I never knew how much," I say to the creek, placing a delicate white agate on my knee.

Then there is music, the depth of his love for it. Concerts, festivals, CDs, DVDs, and *Austin City Limits*, but no limit to that love. Asa sits in a recliner between two speakers and lets his soul wash clean, his reward at the end of the day. I must dance from wall to wall when the volume pounds, but he can no more move about than a surfer planted on his board. Going with the waves: this too pre-dates the merger known as us. From a pile just below the surface I pull a narrow cylinder of glistening chert that could fly as svelte as sound waves do.

And finally, how is it that I married a man so fixated on football? I agreed to attend one game. In the parking lot, I took a blow to the head by a fan's errant pigskin; in the stands I tried to follow the game but could only see the knocking-down of men by other men, and the occasional speck of a ball soaring through goalposts to evoke a thrill among tens of thousands that puzzled me no end. Asa sat enthralled by the ritual, the crowd's one mind, the titillation of potential injury while the seated are safe and all eyes. I don't get it, but don't have to. "I can't tell his boy's heart not to go," I explained to a swatch of moss, looking for a miniature football-shaped rock for my collection.

Three stones, precious as any gems, pocketed. Why do I stay with him? Because the man is alive, has passions, and is not all work and no play. The creek advised: *look closely at what is really loved in those you judge before you judge.*

I walked further into the woods then, veered to the pond that never got repaired. The stone-gathering and new views on Asa fueled euphoria. But it was always a letdown: the pond with so much potential was a big bowl with a giant crack. It was never going to be the family swimming hole I'd pictured.

I peered straight into the cleft where the dam gaped. It was rumored the former owners were lousy at constructing ponds; there were three on the land, all of them worthless, though one made a shallow drinking-hole for deer when the rain stayed on. Here was a secluded and magical dip in the hills for which my plans had been fierce. The pond could have been a shining secret deep in the land. Its northern edge, a steep climb, bordered Up Top, and all around its circumference the trees were some of the land's tallest, whose roots might have benefitted from the vessel filling up. It was a dream that never manifested—one of many that slid into impossibility after mother-death, miscarriages, autism, and the words among us.

I forced myself to stare at the hole and mourn the pond I'd never re-invent. I thought of the troubled family that owned this land before us and suddenly missed my dad—he, too, was a grand

and sterling promise, but there was a hole in our relationship that grew the more I did.

My dad and I started out intact when I was little, another chip off the old block. He lived large inside his profession and assumed that was his gift to us—the moxie to speak truth to power. But when I began that shaky quest for a separate self, we clashed constantly. I was critical, as teenagers are, and he rejected me, contemptuous and dismissive.

He might have studied what it was like to be the establishment for once—he who thrilled to rebel against the rules of academia—but he threw me away as a traitor turning more seditious with each challenge to his authority. I washed out from the hole in the dam and fought my way through the wilderness of my life without the guide that could have been a worthy candidate for the job. Dear Old Dad.

But these days someone else is Daddy Man. That's what the girls and I call Asa in the house. I may have started it. His favorite daughter glommed onto the phrase, while the silent watcher of a girl can only manage *Dad*. In the daily-ness of our lives, I most often addressed my husband in familiar shorthand—*Babe*. But now and again, with no context, Daddy Man slips out from between my lips.

I wouldn't be the first woman with those kinds of issues, and the phantom-pond wasn't judging me. But it shocked me to discover how much I expected Asa never to falter.

Ever.

In the early days of our marriage, he used to ask, so seriously, if he had to be strong all the time? *No*, I reassured him, with my own career, my money generated, my generous parents, my clients, and my research. I found the question dear for what it cost him to ask, but slightly silly. We were feminists, weren't we? We would both be of equal strength.

The girls' entrance shifted everything. We planned that I would play house for a year or so, then get back into the swing of working mom. But it never happened. How did we end up so traditionally structured?

The strain of raising a special-needs child is a story untold. Autism presents what only the brethren can hear because your kid's mind and behavior swing so far outside the norm. Yet I've learned more from this ordeal than from any others about compassion and suffering, about justice and how to warrior.

It's not the child's fault that the entire family can end up in a hostage situation. Everything revolves around the uncertainty, the set-apartness, day after day. Someone must withstand the worst of the anguish and the labor, and Asa checked out while doing his monetary duty. The sibling was too young to have responsibility placed on her, so it fell to me.

Nina, the silent and watchful one, echoes me in my family of origin. I was the oddball between two brothers, yes-men to our father's every directive. Unlike me, they dodged his contempt while I deplored their lack of courage. My mother, his acolyte, tried to frown me down and stuck firmly to his side. In that family I was the one out of step, and I was let go for that. I would not have my daughter suffer a similar fate.

The severity of autism, the lack of any hope for recovery in our oldest wore on Asa and me and was a lot of work from the start. We were in the country, miles from services. The nearest small town was a bastion of blue/pink-collar individuals with a smattering of conservative professionals. I was without time or energy to serve the area as a therapist and turned my focus full on my daughter, to the detriment of her sibling—and expected Daddy Man to feed, clothe, and shelter the endeavor *and* be there a hundred percent for me emotionally.

Eventually Asa quit asking if he had to be strong. If I were truthful, I'd admit the answer had changed to *Yes, because I do.* But I must have hoped he would be the industrious *and* available father

I never had, one to admire and applaud my sacrifice, and lift me up with affection and gratitude.

Only out on the land could I separate myself from this daughter who was the outcast and father-forsaken mirror of me. But back in the fray she brought me out of myself with what she taught about the epidemic that most didn't want to see: these strange kids grunting without language, smearing feces on the walls, tortured by the screech of discordant sound and the scrape of most textures. Asa grasped this deeply. He saw a travesty across our nation, enacted locally in our home, and like me the knowledge set him apart from his peers—but court and hearings and the office were the solace he turned to, just as I turned to the land. I faulted him for not pulling with me, refusing to join forces to love this young one and to show it like I did. He couldn't handle it. Autism. Her.

So, a man let me down again, in the person of my children's father, we the late bloomers who picked parenting while others picked out colleges for their progeny. He let me down when he chose the easy one for his favorite and walled off the outcast. Even when he knew that nothing, especially not autism, was ever her fault.

Sitting in the dry scoop of pond that never got rewoven, a word seemed to lilt up from the ground, a word laced with promise. The word wasn't in my vocabulary, and I was strongly in a mood to quarrel with it. To me it was—truthfully—puerile. I found it the epitome of weakness. The word was *forgiveness.*

Forgive Asa? After all he'd done? What a simpering idea. I was committed to making a stand, showing my daughters how to be tough. I needed instructions on how to be less wimp and better warrior—especially in the marital struggle, and how to be a more efficient architect of my children's futures. What I received instead was a gentle re-direction as cirrus wisps overhead, a slew of oaks and the cry of a Cooper's hawk advised me to let go.

Let it go.

"But he's wrong! He'll get away with too much! I'll be rubber-stamping what is so against my principles! He'll have carte blanche to do even worse things!"

Do you want peace or to win at war?

Skewered, if carefully regarded, by a non-wrathful force: running away was more than impolite, it was asinine. You don't blow off being personally handled by the gods.

That's when I arrived at my first-ever about-face on the Relationship Repetition Road. Was charging weapons against Asa's injustices getting me anywhere? Were the daughters emboldened or simply made sad? Did I ever win? Did he?

I remembered stumbling onto a blog where the comments women spilled about their husbands creeped me out—as in when you fear you might belong to a familiar subset. The hatred! Over things such as the way he eats, dresses, and of course ignores them except as sexual receptacles. The women were bitter to their core, romance crushed to an acid boil. I didn't cringe because the women's losses were rendered so raw, but because each of them was utterly unable to marshal a shred of free agency—except to believe in the next prince to come. Would he be the Daddy Man they'd always wanted?

I heard myself in their hissing diatribes. They weren't battered women or cornered servants, only lonely, stalemated fighters like me. I felt sorry for every schmo they married who was simply waiting for mom's nice face to come back so he could be the little prince again.

Certainly, Asa was mother-haunted, and I was failing as a substitute. Why is it excusable for a man to wish his wife to be like mom, but weak for a woman to have Daddy Issues? There is no daughter's parallel assertion to *my mother is a saint*. Regardless, it was the first time I chose to see that everybody suffers, and that included Asa.

It made sense that I married an attorney. As a girl I was sensitive to power disturbances in the neighborhood, quick to cry foul of bullies or snobby popular kids or crusty, mean teachers. The Sixties hit me hard. At fourteen I was fed up with the pressure to maintain good-girlism. If only fair would be fair, I believed, utopia would pass from pipedream into solid plan. Where did I retreat to with my teen angst about patent unfairness that seemed everywhere, coming from everyone? I walked the vacant lots and undeveloped edges of university grounds, parks, and riverbanks, where I schemed on how to triumph over the hate.

To marry an attorney—one who told me while we were courting that nature was his church? It was the best of both worlds. Neither of us dreamed we'd end up playing opposing counsel to the other. We faced off deliberately, but at the same time we felt betrayed to see our alliance breached.

Yet it was true: his chosen career implied an inherent safety for me and our daughters. I'd seen the effect of his mystique work on people. I also knew that lawyers could thoroughly divine "the system" and use it from the inside. But Asa was invested in his profession to the point of forgetting he was also a person. I played into it, let it dominate the trajectory of our family, because in some way it spelled S-A-F-E-T-Y. If inside the house there might be soul collision, in the bustling community we would be all right with Daddy Man as our bulwark. We would be spared when others got the shaft. We would prevail in a duel of wits or wanton outrage.

I frequently watched Asa dress in the morning, both mystified and mollified by the sight. The white shirts were buttoned to the neck. The tying of the tie, though often uniquely colorful, chic, or humorous, looked like practice for the gallows. The dress pants and suit coat were of a fabric that repelled me, so unnatural to the touch, navy blue or black. I thought of nuns back in elementary school in their full habits, and how they managed every day to don such drapes. It must have meant the world to them. When you put on a uniform you want to believe in, it changes you, emboldens you, makes you better—and I wish I could believe that.

Daddy Man was a superiority I believed in and feared I could never match, for his sense of duty. I'd never felt duty to anyone before my daughters other than to the oppressed, and to the land. There was no dress uniform to focus my mission outward on these fronts. The main of the mainstream saw autism-parents as shrill dummies who squawked about vaccines; similarly, tree-huggers were shaggy hippies in tents.

Yet there was that word. *Forgiveness.* It irked me because I feared sacrifice, placid victimhood, tongue stayed, and other cheek turned. But the land I trusted, my partner in the real marriage, still posed it: *forgive.* I let the sweet whispers that proposed forgiveness work on me for several minutes, and it felt like watching those slow-motion images of grand old buildings being felled by dynamite. All fall down. If fight fell into forgiveness, what safety, what meaning left in the guerilla uniform I wore that only I could see? The vision of such destruction at once stupefied and sang of renewal.

I knew I was lucky for a chance to halt a fragile ego's long rampage. Would the word gift me enough to examine it?

After the creek handed over petite stones of gratitude and the dam broke about Daddy Man, with the fight nearly drained out of me, I walked still deeper into my woods. Wild gooseberry barely stood back from the deer's winding path; every year I tried to maintain a regular trail until the seasons obliterated it. Still, crashing through beauty I could see and breathe, I felt made special. Because it's all for these eyes, this skin, these pleasure centers.

Others may take morning on their sacred ground, and I hope for them— because for me—nothing exists but their "here." I rarely got up this early; sunrise seems a brash promise that seldom follows through. But for some reason I couldn't sleep. It came clear now: I needed a plan, and I came here to get one.

A haze dressed the early day with burnished softness. The place looked at once lit and muted, like the trick of a smeared lens. A rising sun wasn't pushy but climbed among master artists' creations as the wind played with my hair just the way I like it.

Ahead was a sycamore, a friend and my favorite among trees, bark patched in gray-gold splotches, leaves big enough to cover a baby's head. Bold and beautiful: if I were a tree, I wouldn't be a sycamore. Probably a hackberry, with its raised ridges less spiteful than thorns, but an attempt at defense just in case.

Blue herons nest in sycamores because of sycamores' giant size, up to 175 feet tall. The trees are one of the oldest species on the planet, an elder. I paused under the great canopy for a wisdom moment from a wisdom elder. This tree is not a path-pointer, like water traversing, but a permanently planted voice on my land:

If one side wins, there is no peace, only uneasy and temporary control. It's a sham and the end of marriage, the pact you made.

It was true that I waged a chronic battle of resistance against Asa's ammo: I believed he designed it to disable my self-esteem. Or to remove me into the boonies of relationship where the exchange of affection happened on a sporadic schedule. I starved but to a point: alert to the timing of my near deprivation, he deftly delivered a morsel. How could I prove this was so? If you asked him, he might provide an identical analysis of my dance toward and away. A sprinkle of love, a seed of hope.

But hope failed, a shaky little flyer, too sensitive to the fact of lack. Hope went cold when hunger returned. Could I say to hell with hope and place peace on a pedestal higher than love, whatever that is? How to trash-bin pride enough to embrace truce and revel in a cease-fire?

And what about andropause, aging, and other real-life constructions? What about his turn from the land into his work so thoroughly—was all that really aimed at me? Was I called to do more than take his shortcomings as an affront?

He is your teacher, said the sycamore. *He teaches without putting a foot out here. He doesn't mirror you; he challenges you like a brick wall whose hidden door you've not found yet. Forgiveness is the key that fits the lock.*

It's easier mulling about justice than about love. But love is what I know I can feel for the sycamore and this whole land. I also love my children, innocent as tadpoles. I bear the intrusion of my shame over them seeing me like this, heading for the hills instead of their hearts.

I don't know how to love what seems like a weapon disguised as a man wearing a ring that I put on his finger, a ring that says one thing while we do wholly another. But if I can't inhabit the ground of my soul—with or without his permission—I will forever be plotting revenge, obsessing about the lack of respect I reap. The land will remain impassive in the face of my holding pattern, my daughters learning darkly that peace is never possible.

Whither the Borderline badge that certifies he's twisted, and I'm caught in the wake? So easy and ready-made. And who says I don't do my part, along with work and financial pressures, to keep him in that diagnosis-box? Where was my label—I'd had a couple, nothing now, but when do they expire?

I turned in a full circle. All I saw were trees holding onto this land. Some had taken hits from microbursts or lightning. Some were deceased and leaning in the crooks of their brethren or flat on the ground, returning to the soil that once uplifted them. In the heart of the Pause there was a time that I grew so tired of people, I decided that when forced to endure a crowd I'd look only at trees instead of humans. Because usually there they were, stately and silent, revealing themselves vigilant and determined.

These trees on "my" land were no more "mine" than the clouds that floated over. I would attempt to follow their counsel. They said things that never would have occurred to me on my own, although the denizens of therapy would look to the subconscious or, if brave, the collective unconscious and say that I tapped a vein. I feared I lacked the courage to put down my weapons. Then something gave way in the cage of my heart, and the tears were of refreshment, not resentment. I had everything to gain from a sea-change within, whether or not Asa paid me back in kind.

"Sycamore, mi amor, will you help me carry this tenderness out of the woods and into the house?"

May Contempt Falter

May contempt fall to contempt for itself. May it disembowel its own haughty anaerobes.

May such immolation end in pity for the desperate blunders it made.

May contempt, the deadliest of the Four Horsemen, stand as the Grand Mistake. For contempt is a blanket too easily spread over the bed of all relationships.

Contempt is co-efficient in the shelter of superiority. As we blaze on high, those below are surely the stupid, the rubes, the willfully ignorant, knee-jerked by the first words that pop into their heads. How we hate stupid. *They bring this on themselves,* we fume, for the stupid must not prevail. Contempt offers a tactic, learned through bully-schemes that grew out of playground diminishments. It was no child's mistake. It was the way of the world spelled out plain, and you were far too free to say to another kid what you held back from the big people.

When the marriage partner you took to your hand, your heart, and your spirit resorts to elaborate thumb-wrestling, contempt is the tool to angle for position. May all marriages and lovers be wiped of superiority (the sneer, the words among us) and the out-and-out duel. Where the loser crumples to one booby prize, and that is humiliation. Stuck with that tar, losers start scouting for revenge.

Contempt always keeps score.

Sycamore, how many knife stabs does it take to shake the phantom-limb pain, to dissolve into the truth of our human horribleness and find the best response. *Feeling with?* How long before I realize I'm not the queen who can forever prevent mean? Stay safe in the bower of unconditional love? Getting mean about the ravages of mean somehow fails to bring justice. Marriage is conditional love anyway, highly so. Divorce is the common triage. *People come and people go.*

When I am in the envelope of spousal disdain, may I leave the playground finally. Say the finishing words: *I will not fight with you.* Let him sleep it off, take it to work, swallow one more OCD Borderline irritation in the corona of habit. I can't change him. But I can pray: *dearest antidote, forgiveness, please enter my home.*

Contempt, you rub me raw, but what if I step aside from your one track? You then have no oomph. I believe in your demise when I refuse your obstacle course, when I weave shields against the flying dirt that wants to get up in my brain, the emotional brain.

And you, forgiveness, I'm in. Let's get started. Step one: ban contempt from my modus, one that boomerangs too often. No weapons allowed when the other's self-contempt wings toward my many Achilles's heels. Nor will I be a willing target, intent on brownie points for being good, turning the other cheek. What is the way, then, to finally break this Horseman down to a trotter with no mean mouth?

First—forgive me for what I have done to myself, for I knew not what I did.

Book Three

18

I sat at the computer in our bedroom. Asa, across the hall, stared at television with the girls; everyone was hooked on the Beverly Hillbillies classics out on DVD. I didn't notice how suddenly he stood up. I registered his approach, hoping he'd veer to the kitchen. I didn't know that Asa had just seen the television screen shrink from forty-six inches to twelve. That he sat mesmerized as the entire screen continued to wither to a box so tiny he could no longer see the actors or sets. That he stared at a screen that wasn't blurry or dark, only miniature.

My husband walked into the hallway. Neither woozy nor weak, just feeling strange. It wasn't a long hall. To him it stretched a hundred feet. That's when he came to me and ran down the figures on the shrinking TV.

"Let's get some air," I said, hiding the fact that I was vexed to be torn from my writing, my mind around it like a vice, snipping at sentences until they stood strong. I had a tough time focusing on what I believed was another of Asa's anxiety attacks, his persistent plague.

He'd gotten better though. No longer was he prone to stopping his vehicle along a freeway exchange when the curve rose blind like a drop to nowhere, walking up the perilous shoulder until he could see that the road really did continue its downhill slope. Change had made the rounds in his mind, prompted by his own Pause. He'd slowed the pace of work. No longer sleeping mostly in hotel rooms, waking hourly to adjust the temperature and check the alarm on the digital clock, he had calmed overall. Andropause cancelled his airport habit. He didn't like going anywhere now, having moved his office entirely into our home. Still, little time was spent with tools in the garage or putzing in the garden. He was safe before the television, or when a client came in much worse off than he thought he'd ever be.

Was this the return of Odysseus? When Asa could no longer cope as a travelling barrister, he came finally and fully to live at home and we adjusted, attaining a hard-won romantic camaraderie. We worked out the worst of things. Not so often were big mouths the problem, with their by-products of criticism and contempt when he shot forth and I fired back. I studied forgiveness in the literature, avoiding what was faith-based, and it blossomed in me as a commitment, if a shaky ability. Both daughters relaxed in our presence. Over the course of our twenty years together, enmity and backbiting waxed and waned, but eventually there were fewer, less heated outbursts and longer recovered periods.

It was reason to stay. Hadn't I dwelled in the dark and doom long enough? I took to making a daily gratitude list: the rule was to log at least ten items, no matter how small, but they had to be heartfelt.

This is what being a student of forgiveness brought. Not the feared doormat status, but a softening of heart. Relief. The cessation of re-played images from the disappointing past made for breathing room. There was a lot more cognizance for this moment, this man, this family, these dreams of mine.

And although as menopause slowly slipped off to bother someone else and I longed to be filled and fucked royally on Sunday mornings, the closeness meant more, and such, I heard and believed, was the essence of marriage. Big deal if the parts don't work the way they used to. This happens when you get older. At least he was home, and as I gloried in the about-face, I missed the red flag: there were obvious signs his health was failing. I must have still believed in an unspoken hope that Daddy Man would be forever strong.

I left my desk that night to accompany him. On the porch, dusk was rolling to dark. It was November but warm as a summer's eve. That wouldn't last long. Asa expressed a desire to have sex, which got my attention. Not because I was in the headspace for it but because now I knew something was wrong. When anxious, he wasn't amorous. This decidedly didn't fit the pattern of his usual panic attack. And what the hell was with the shrinking television?

He didn't seem scared. I was baffled, tracking his sensations, but with a hint of awe that infused the moments. I didn't want to believe anything was as wrong as it turned out to be.

Long have I pondered this intercession of sexual desire into the unfolding of a stroke. I've read others' experience and don't see it anywhere. But now I understand.

An inside account of one massive brain-bleed is Jill Bolte Taylor's *My Stroke of Insight.* She marvels at stroke's silver lining, the ability to feel an incredible oneness with the universe as the minutiae of schedules and responsibility slips away, not to be retrieved by language (gone) or judgment (all is relative). When the two hemispheres of the brain surrender their stand-off, the result is, according to Taylor, an understanding about the nature of life so hugely important it rivals the impact of a near-death experience.

As a result, the fully recovered, Harvard-trained neuroanatomist writes that never, post-stroke, does she let piddly-ass stress or negativity into her psyche, her body, or her environment. Never. Because she knows—due to stroke—that sweating the small stuff is a costly burden to a human life. When the author's mother arrives at the hospital shortly after her daughter is admitted into Intensive Care, this is the scene:

> She looked me straight in the eye and came right to my bedside. She was gracious and calm, said her hellos to those in the room, and then lifted my sheet and proceeded to crawl into bed with me. She immediately wrapped me up in her arms and I melted into the familiarity of her snuggle. It was an amazing moment in my life.

I believe that in our stroke-unfolding, night-porch moment, Asa responded instinctively to the need to be held by another person—even though he could still speak, walk, plot, and compare. Stroke's propensity to unlock the brain from its normal duties goes beyond sending it on the likes of an LSD trip: *if we are all one, hold me close to your animal warmth.* I wish I had understood this at the time, for I took umbrage at his horniness, certain he should be telling me to take him to the hospital instead.

He would not reveal that he thought he was dying. Over and over I urged and cajoled: "The emergency room. Let's go!"

Repeatedly, he refused. "It's the caffeine."

Two days earlier, he'd quit his six daily cups of coffee. Cold turkey. No tapering, no Cokes to ease the separation, one big headache to bear. Should have been no problem there! Caffeine consumption is correlated with stroke. But quitting so suddenly, after decades of severe addiction? The brain just had to say *Whoa!*

Doctors shrugged that off when thirty-six hours later I firmly told Asa's shaken and weary shell that we were bound for the Emergency Room. He was admitted at once and pronounced in atrial fibrillation, an abnormal heart rhythm that can lead to a vascular accident. Every scan and test confirmed it: hemorrhagic stroke, the little clot that could.

I felt this coming, as Asa became more rotund and sedentary, as November tightened around us with its any-day-now dreary temperatures, and its edicts to holiday cheer. And yet. We were in a good place. I believed my conversion with the sycamore and others cured a trend toward catastrophe, including any failing health that was coming for him. My dogged switch to peace instead of the words among us: how did it happen? We talked. But this time, I brought the land into it. I told all.

I told Asa what the sycamore said. How things talked to me out there. I risked it—I never had before. And, to my great relief, he paused and considered. He thought maybe it was the voice of something like God. Or, to him: Justice. The blind lady with the scales aloft. She was Holy Mother in his eyes.

He wrote to me. A letter that bled a little, line after line. About how much he hurt from the arrows I sent flying when his contempt trotted its paces between us. How sorry he was that he had loved the ghost of his mother too long. How tentatively he longed to be closer to the silent daughter and stop monopolizing the happy-mascot's time, who was getting increasingly surly at us anyway. How we could beat this, our adversity. Andropause curled in on itself and wanted detente.

I thought I could do that.

But why didn't peace ward off this blow to the brain? What did he further have to abdicate: the male breadwinner mode? It makes some men sick. Why couldn't he see I was holding up my end? And as for money, his barometer, I bought nothing for me, except in thrift stores. I favored library books and learned to throw weeds in the salad: dandelion, purslane, chickweed. What else did I need? Time to traipse the land pacifistic, and it was all mine.

The land asked, *did you reconcile because you wanted a reward?* It asked me to think about testing, and what I was made of now.

To the abdicating brain I said: I will seek to machete through your brambles. I will hunt for the man in there, the one I used to know. I have been schooled by the brain that fell to "autism," that silly word, for it speaks only of "self," as if those in that prison don't long to get out. Now hear this: no brain gets by *me.*

19

I wish I could forget the look on Asa's face as an orderly helped him into the car after the stroke mandated a hospital stay. He walked into the place but left in a wheelchair. In those three days he turned from Daddy Man into an invalid, and November threw an ice storm over every surface outdoors. As we made to leave the hospital, I saw his bald terror—of me. What had I done? I was merely intent on getting him out of there, with the same fervor I'd wanted him in. If the doctors said *go*, then surely home was the best medicine.

Despite his weak demeanor I clung to a faith in how lucky he fared. This was the stroke that fooled us at first.

Because when the television shrank and the hallway seemed to stretch into the next county, Asa was adamant he was only wrestling with a panic attack. After we left the front deck, discarding the idea that sex would override his anxiety, he convinced me of the Caffeine Theory regarding his strange state. I went back to my desk, he to his shrunken screen. I glanced frequently across the hall: he was levitating his arms to check for paralysis every five minutes. "I'm not having a stroke," he called from the recliner. He walked up and down the hallway, straight as an arrow. "It's not a stroke."

Yet what of the vision loss? Asa dropped this bombshell at my doorway: "I can't see from here (forty-five-degree angle from his right side) to here (arm straight out to the side)."

"That's it," I rose. "Emergency room."

"I will *not!*" He fled back to the recliner, where it would be impossible to pry him loose for the rest of the evening.

The next day he slept. All day.

Well, calling caffeine quits is a real energy drain, I told myself, pulling the household weight as if he were on an airplane, bound to a legal hearing.

The following morning was Monday. One daughter left in her special-needs van. The other readied for our drive to a different school. Asa didn't look well. I could smell fear of the unknown, and it was contagious.

He walked to the driveway, shaken and pale. No paralysis, no problem with speech, "I can walk and talk. But I don't feel right."

"Get in the car," I said.

It was early and he had the Emergency Room all to himself. Once the tests were conclusive, they didn't treat him like a man who'd gotten off easy. With the donning of hospital gown, the gluing and probing of monitor wires and the procession of specialists into the room, he looked a person I'd never seen before.

I was afraid to be afraid.

20

Uses for a stroke:

    1.   You can see a client the day you come home from the hospital and observe the grinding effort it takes to make sense of what comes out of their mouths.

    2.   You can walk into open cabinet doors, store displays, and parked cars because the other day you misplaced a swath of your vision that tracks objects and motion.

    3.   You can mourn the fact that you will lose your place repeatedly inside the pages of a book, even a great one.

    4.   You can only recline before the television or under the sleep-apnea mask because the act of making a living for one portion of each day has drained your energy to the barrel's bottom.

    5.   You will never again play the song that reminds you how much you love your wife.

6. You can turn away from the fact that everything you thought you held dear feels like
ashes in your brain. You feel guilty: you had a
stroke, you're not what you once were, you let
everyone down. You're angry because they
don't get that.

Nonetheless, it was hard not to make Asa's stroke all about me.

I had a spike in my head, too: the belief that he had to have
seen this coming. The extra pounds, the sedentariness. The snoring
punctuated by in-held breath. The isolation from all but persons
who paid him. The blood-pressure meds that no longer worked.
The disinclination to exercise or renew his energy, the refusal to
listen to me about any of that.

Soon enough, I saw the fulfilling of the contract to end up like
Mom with her stroke and thereby vindicate her. The doctors pronounced a new find: diabetes. Just like Mom. It's horrid to admit,
but I was pissed.

I took this out on his medical staff at the hospital, when I
should have been curled around him like Jill Bolte Taylor's mom. I
thought I was doing the right thing. I mistrusted the drugs and ex-
traneous procedures and positioned myself as his advocate—un-
smiling and stiff and without compassion. Resorting to control
while circumstances cried *no control possible here!*

I turned over and over in my mind how he manifested this
scary turn of events. How it was going to ruin my life. What about
our daughters? He'd had so little energy before. Now he would be
drained. Because each day he spent in the Intensive Care Unit he
looked weaker and worse. I hoped it was what holistic practitioners
called "the healing crisis": symptoms take a nosedive before they
improve—although his care was anything but holistic. As he slept
the sleep that brought no restoration, I waited, was present to our
daughters, forsook the great outdoors. Asa woke to work, he ate,
then fell back to dreamland. Inch by inch he interacted more, but

who was this person? Not the one who'd made a loving truce with me.

The peace we'd settled into swiftly left the atmosphere of our marriage. Asa now had a pressing need to use work for a lifeline. He cited how many of his clients noted a similar uproar with their spouses post-stroke: we had to get used to this new norm, I gathered, even if we were aging lovebirds before it hit. No matter that we'd just reached a level of comfortable romance, where I had listened to what the land said about forgiveness, and he responded by learning to value my presence and personality. It was true; things in the space between sycamore and stroke did wax into something better, solid, and even keeled. Peace was attained, although at some price.

The day Asa went to the hospital was a crucial day for me and my new business. I had decided to re-brand myself from therapist to life coach and invited another with the same moniker to give classes with me on nutrition and mental health. I'd learned much about diet and supplementation, the effect of a troubled gut on the brain, which eased Nina's distress—applied to my own migraines and anxiety, the results were significant in terms of energy, clarity, and optimism. I'd carried on this study with household duties plus the ecosexual affairs with my land and other spots that I haunted. It was worth sharing with others, and high time.

I met my partner in the endeavor, who I was beginning to loathe, at the hospital to discuss her need to carry the night's presentation alone. She had another agenda and not a word about my husband's stroke. The incident elaborated the surreal salad that stroke was quickly tossing my way.

We sat in her car in the hospital parking lot. To be fair, I voiced my disapproval of Asa and how he brought his demise upon himself. It was hardly a plea for sympathy, though she might have acknowledged my distress. I glanced sideways at her new hairdo, one of many, and marveled at the clothes, too. This time she had gone complete middle-class-mom. The unnatural mass covering her head was Fifties bouffant; the weensy curls upturned at the cheeks spoke housewifely decorum. A suit of the most bulky and conservative cut hung on her frame. Gone were the revealing little black dresses she'd chosen every other night. I didn't have much time to ponder it; my mind was in the hospital room as she launched into her diatribe.

Last time we'd talked she'd asked for a critique of her solo practice as a relationships coach. The utter chaos that marked her life prompted a few questions on my part. When I'd spoken about narcissism, a subject intimately connected to the Borderline predicament, she found it brutal. She had pressed me for complete and total honesty—why was I so stupid to provide it?

Now she'd re-grouped, turned into June Cleaver, and consulted a social-worker friend who scoffed at the idea. Her? Narcissistic? Whoever said such a thing? My soon-to-be-ex business partner listed her evidence to counter the verdict of Ultra-Self-Absorption as I simply stared. I wanted to say many things. *Hey, my man is in that building possibly dying from uncontrollable high blood pressure and ascending insulin havoc, and you are not a narcissist for making this speech right now?*

I kept running home to handle the kids; Asa had just hired a new assistant: *welcome to work, your boss had a stroke.* I needed to appear in control, so the young thing didn't bolt. The land was a half hour's drive from the hospital along winding gravel, and the girls were in two different schools. Asa kept saying I wasn't there with him in the hospital enough.

This is what happens when you close yourself into a marriage with only the land to fully see you. There isn't a safety net for the caregiver, a role I knew already too well due to our special-needs child. I worried that the workload was about to double. What good would come of it?

If You Think I'm Praying Now

Think again.

Cram the last straw down my throat and see what I abandon: faith, belief, forbearance. God doesn't give you more than you can handle? Tell the Queen of Heaven I can't talk right now.

The brain presents as a creaky machine, not the crowning glory where mystics process their ecstasy and aloneness. The brain of the beloved, no matter how many horsemen proceeded to drag their hooves through the spaces between us, entered some unnamable sync with mine the first time we made love—which must necessitate on some level, that mine got pinged by the stroke. I felt fuzzy, as if I didn't know anything.

But like the television screen, I shrank to the tasks at hand, which distinguished me from "the stroke victim."

The amazing thing, for better or worse, was the saving of his speech. Asa maintained language without slur or hesitation. No vocabulary was siphoned off to the salvage yard, maybe or maybe not to be retrieved. The doctor said, "You had so much brain power to begin with, that's what."

Words among us in the days following stroke: everything's unsaid. I won't say it, don't say it, only focus on his comfort and recovery. Be there, let him fill the whole vista today, and there is only today.

The land erotic? It can wait.

21

Asa returned to lawyering and soldiered on, as if the stroke was a bad dream. He had to write down every drop of information a client told him. When driving, he asked whoever was in the passenger seat to watch his right side. He was perpetually irritated at me. He scoffed at the finding of diabetes, forgoing finger-pokes and monitors, and kept loading up on sugar and carbs. He wouldn't hear of regular check-ups, exercise, or dedicated stress management.

Later that summer I contracted what seemed like the flu, but it wouldn't go away. The fatigue was crushing, the fever unrelenting. My thoughts were a ramble toward despair, and eventually a *so what?* attitude toward dying. Two weeks and I was no better. This was novel, for I knew how quickly I kicked a bug. I went to a doctor whom I'd heard was alternative-medicine friendly. He was perplexed. Then he freaked out.

The fever wouldn't come down. The doctor had blood drawn and it was normal. "Patients like this usually go to the Emergency Room," he said, harried, and strangely I appreciated his honest lack of confidence. I was wiped out; he was talking about a spinal tap. Then: "maybe you have Lyme Disease."

That plague allegedly raged only on the coasts but what if it arrived as the vindication of Asa's tick-horror on land left to burgeon wild for two decades? Lyme disease. It could be carried through woodland to a bite upon flesh via the beautiful, the gentle, the majestic deer.

I researched and talked to Lyme advocates: there is no test that can confirm you *don't* have it. False negatives and false positives abound. Don't heap blame on the deer—any warm-blooded mammal can carry the black-legged biter. I also learned that Lyme asserts itself everywhere, inland as well as the coasts.

The body shouts truth if we listen with great care. An animal instinct told me not to believe hypochondria was the root of this malaise. It took trust to read the signs that Lyme's spiral bacteria undulated through my bloodstream.

I investigated plants and supplements. By twists and turns, I came across a weed called Teasel, and it worked.

The only method I had to confirm that my symptoms were Lyme was how markedly I responded to the plants known to trounce Lyme. I added Japanese knotweed, a noxious invader that has enough resveratrol to foil a heart attack or the onset of Alzheimer's. Also, to round out the trio at which Lady Teasel presides, a queen of renown: the Amazon River basin's herb known as Cat's Claw. She can slap an immune system into shape like nobody's business. Together, with some ginseng for energy, these healers snatched me from the deathly sleep.

I ordered from a small herbalist who tinctured the Teasel on her farm, then a company that sells Chinese herbs. For a long while it was just Teasel and me. She never let me down. Dipascus in botany-speak, Xu Duan in Chinese—to me she means No Teasing. Within a week, I was back in the pink.

Asa made it past stroke with three days in the hospital and an immediate return to work. He never fully believed I had Lyme since there was no test. It wasn't like the stroke: no circle of specialists and well-worn routines in the temples of allopathy. But anyone could see that without these plants, I was less. Far less. Sometimes, when I tested their power by forsaking them, it wasn't mere brain fog that returned. A day seemed like climbing a sheer cliff with a backpack of granite and me with no muscle, joints, or strong bones to bear up.

With a house and kids to attend to, I couldn't afford to be sick. Nor could I fully face the symbolism talking in my illness. The big giveaway that something was terribly wrong was the tenor of depression—a flat line of no affect, not the sobs of my youth or active hopelessness inside replays of past stupidities, and I could have cared less what Asa said or didn't say. In a way, I thank Lyme's depression for its frank and uncluttered wasteland that let me hear its death-friendly feelings as code: *take heed! Do something!*

I stuck to Teasel and company because they gave me life while Asa collected prescriptions, allowing the deleterious effects to accumulate, changing him skeletally, and changing him emotionally. He looked warily across the gap left by our choices. I longed to understand: did he accept his "chronic condition" as part of a lineage, trawling toward death because that's what Mom did? Or did the medications craft a culturally-specific kind of depression— Pharma's complicity with the masculine wound that demands stoicism and struggling on, for this defines a man?

I tried out this argument on Asa. He looked at me and I saw the way his eyelids drooped at the corners, the pure white beard with skin so sallow, although the eyes were still a heartbreaking blue. "Would you please—" he started.

But the words among us failed. Bringing up Saint Mom and his own stroke in the same breath was heresy, and trying to ladle shame for toxic-male work-horsing when work was all he had? Sensing the arrival of one of the Four Horsemen—Contempt—I instinctively drew back. Why couldn't I see that there was a new rider glued to yet another precarious saddle? Its name was Fear.

Humbled by The Weed

I sing praise to the "bottle brush" of roadsides, seeps, and sedge meadows. Teasel, prickly in nature, grows as tall as a human. It is called an invader, creeper, destroyer of crops and natives. What a taproot, girl! Two feet down and still thrusting!

I love her.

Among medicinal plants Teasel is silky when rendered to a light brown powder, Chinese-herb style. Such softness to her milk-chocolate pulvil that even the side of your finger sweeping off a teaspoon feels it. To open the jar to her scent is to imbibe both woodland and a fragrance so exotic at first, I didn't know whether to puke or inhale. Now I'm in love. Because without her, I lose. Lady Teasel, I don't even know where you live on my land, if at all. I have heard you are shy by nature. Some call you noxious and plot to stymie your spread. Others gather and decoct you as you have instructed, and I am among the grateful.

How do I tell anyone about you, about the power of one plant, let alone shake them into grasping the mystery of a ditch-grower who gives swift balm to the course of an illness? Is it all chance that some weeds grow with potent healing ability ignored for their "invasiveness?" What if we were schooled to plant them, each household or neighborhood, to share when needed, or for prevention of disease that gets to be a bigger deal when it's not called out for its true name?

Oh Lady, you are so misunderstood and reviled. Yet how I owe you. If ever I could see your delicate petals—five, just like my fingers—stretched out to cup each rosette you fill with hundreds of seeds, I would stop right there and build a shrine. I would give you to the world, like a parent at the altar handing their offspring to the beloved: *be fruitful!*

How the tall and sassy garner the urges to snip them down! How they suffer the rampages of the war against their vitality! Lady, come to my garden but know that I, too, will have to contain you. Yes, if you will work with me, you may be restrained in number, but not destroyed. Join our human community, and we will talk to and coddle you, make sure nutrients grace your leaves and deep-plunging sensor.

When I was healed, I was released. The land erotic welcomed me back, and now I am mad to see you somewhere, standing in a frowsy meadow, vibrating your reluctant welcome to which I say, "Please come home with me!"

22

When relationships are determined by manipulation, by the need for control, they may possess a dreary, bickering kind of drama, but they cease to be interesting. They are repetitious; the shock of human possibility has ceased to reverberate through them.

ADRIENNE RICH

The words among us were back for yet another round but ceased to be interesting. Stroke on top of menopause meant I could no longer cry about the whirlwind of Mean—our tired scripts dried up my well for good. Asa's stroke left him with monotonous, limited responses, which trained my battering ram to keep going for the same spot. We were locked in place.

So long ago, when I was a newlywed bedding down as Asa's parents jousted beyond the short hallway, I was repelled and wished to block my ears. Why didn't I eavesdrop to get the goods on my new in-laws? Because it was repetitive and uninteresting. True, stroke had stripped inflection from Lorene's voice. But even Pops went to his lines as if rote—a part played too long, shot through with an allegiance to the show. *Erase You, Defend My Self.* I'd like to think old marrieds who trade vicious for viciousness might do so because down deep, they hope for "the shock of human possibility" to return and "reverberate" through them. They don't see they are caulking every crack where light could sneak in—with their boredom, their fatigue, the uniformity with which word after predictable word of complaint and condemnation ensure that creative sparks—not to mention the vulnerabilities of love—will sequester in the fanciful tales of romance on the big screen.

I returned to what was ever constant: twenty years after staking a claim on the land erotic, I kept throwing myself to the soft earth to become a different person. Most often I *was* a different person out there—because it was always interesting, devoid of manipulation. Animals and plants do try to control each other all the time—they compete, brutalize, and kill—but is this shaped by resentment and bored habit? Or is the dance of predation a colossal balancing act for ultimate order? Why is it in our human natures to be short, surly, and manipulative? Because of words. They throw off the syzygy.

How to learn a way beyond words? Sit down, look around, and become. When I returned to the house, I was always noticeably calm. Hence my family gave their blessings for me to go and greeted my return with freshened faces of their own.

≈

My Pause waned into a night sweat or two. Andropause eclipsed by stroke was in full swing for Asa. I saw no choice but to

function like the proverbial dried-up prune. Not just a married cel-
ibate, but a bitter soul.

The land was mute. The sycamore towered over brush too
dense for me to risk more Lyme. I drew a conclusion that those
acres were tired of my whining anyway. I should have been learning more about stroke, but I trusted—I needed—Daddy Man to
make the right choices for himself. I knew he was strong enough:
he could still be there for clients in the courtroom, couldn't he?

It's not the end of the world to allow elders a certain cranky
way with the truth. I appreciate it in others. When it came to my
scorn for sex in the days of Asa's health-demise, it was purely sour
grapes piggybacked onto the aging thing. I wondered how I had
chased pants for all those years. I wondered how I ever let Asa bang
away at me. I wondered why anyone would participate in such a
waste of time. It was the outlook of the Pause all over again, but
hadn't I passed through that phase? When would the hot-to-trots
resurge as promised? Who, but the land, would welcome them?

I worried that my thoughts affected our youngest teenager,
dismayed by early pregnancies among her peers. Could I have
transferred my distaste for sex and my repressed obsession about it
to her mind? Once our princess of personability, she now clearly
found her parents abhorrent. Not only could she no longer bear a
hug, but she always needed a ten-foot radius of space. To compare
notes with other moms was highly cathartic for me: blaming teens
for their high drama diverted our pain, made sure we didn't cross-
examine our own failings.

After his big event I thought I'd serve the family best by urging
Asa onto the stroke-recovery bandwagon, and initially he seemed
game. I researched supplements that put the brain back together.
We spent hours with his acupuncturist, and it helped. He played
computer games to challenge memory and focus. On the surface it
looked like a valiant effort. But in time, Asa fashioned a determined

grip on the medication cocktail. To him, only its two-toned pills conferred life.

There were layers to this.

One, neither conventional nor holistic practitioners were able to confront a problem head-on and titrate down the scary meds. I certainly didn't have the expertise. Secondly, the terror of having another stroke made Asa cling to whatever "real doctors" said. Lastly, enter his paranoia that I was trying to control him with diet and supplements. Maybe even kill him.

Oh.

Asa had served a passel of clients disabled by strokes. He read their medical records; he entered the courts of administrative law and won them their due benefits. Hence, he believed it was business as usual when he found me a thorn in his side, a trigger for his anger each time I opened my mouth. Guilty about how brittle I was when he was in the hospital, coupled with worry over his rejection of a holistic healing of the brain, I ramped up efforts to cure his post-stroke malaise the way I'd wrestled with autism when our oldest succumbed. I was on a mission, and it wasn't appreciated.

The words among us were old hat, yet they still went for broke. Asa had little patience and no storage of energy. Exiles who suddenly found themselves in charge again, the words were emboldened by stroke, and they were repetitive, manipulative, and tedious. They reasoned they had every right to stride among the ruin Asa feared for his mind. How did the Borderline pattern fit? How do different damages share the stage, or do they?

We were back to square one, when the marriage struggled with the Four Horsemen daily. Those riders returned uglier now, and their ponies were older. Asa defined himself as a person who'd had a stroke; so, I suppose, as the healthy one, I was an object of envy. He was blunt when I tried to serve up the ideas of exercise, healthy food, or the next new supplement: "complainer," "nag," "bitch" were among the hurled words. He'd never stooped that low before. The fires of contempt he used to set had a devious rationale, but they weren't crude. The Stroke always took the blame for bad language.

When I went to the woods it was with dryness of heart, and only after a hard freeze that nixed the threat of ticks. I had given up the new business—stroke victim plus special-needs child equaled too much to do. I took a steady job in town, beneath my training and experience, when Asa's anger about my lack of earnings reached a crescendo. On some level he was preparing to die, and I knew that. He wanted me to have good benefits and a retirement plan. I thought it would make him happy, and it did seem to ameliorate his contempt for a while, plus earn our younger daughter's respect.

After the daily stint in town, it was back to the land's circle where I did re-learn to weep. I wept because Asa was returning to much earlier war games from our relationship, but with a dangerous overlay. He barely chose to make eye contact, responding neither to cuddles nor pillow-talk. The overriding impression was that he hated me enduringly.

His walk became a shuffle. He seemed scared of the outdoors. He let the hair grow out of his nose and ears. There was the considerable effort to get through the day, his energy more faded than the jeans he took to wearing to the office. Before long, his favorite daughter was contemptuous of him for "not doing *anything*." More than once he tried to explain that he felt he'd let himself down, thus everyone else, too. We couldn't hear that. We just wanted him back.

Grief and great weariness closed the channel to deer mysteries and hawk's overhead call for me. I still appreciated them, but I was no longer touched to the core.

There is a connection between sorrow and Eros in that both throttle one's foundation. Years of steps toward closeness, then away, were rough. Sometimes closeness was better, and finally a plateau into okay developed, which was good. Connected. But this? Odysseus was appalled as cannibals and monsters destroyed his crew one by one until he was the only sailor left, shipwrecked alone on a friendless shore.

As a year post-stroke gained on two, the inner argument I'd wrestled with over the years returned with ferocious needling. *Should I stay or should I go?*

It came down to survival. I reasoned that Asa was plunging with full awareness toward a certain death: the blood pressure would not come down, unhealthy food was loaded without caution, the gym was paid for but unvisited. If I stayed—unwelcome, despised, the only thing he had to fight against—I would succumb to something awful, too, where sadness would wear out my heart, my immune system, and my ability to think clearly. I could feel this foreboding in my flesh daily: the anxious knotted muscles with which I greeted first light, the dread of exodus from the land for an eight-hour shift in town. A pall fell in the house where the air congealed thick with all the potentially healing conversations slated for later.

There was also the issue of Lyme. Though teasel and her crew put me back together, I developed a strange fear of my sacred ground. I feared being re-infected, so found myself going less and less often to the trees and rarely to the deep woods. It's not that I faulted the land. The reasons for the spread of Lyme are complicated and far-reaching, but the irony is intense: I was bitten and made ill with the help of the very creatures I venerate, white-tailed deer who weave their daily rounds close to the house, who only congregate on these acres because so many habitats elsewhere are paved by gentry with an appetite for houses and shopping malls.

At last, a decision was made.

Penance

What is the penance, what is the fine, the fee to be free? Who am I longing for, the one true one?

Not the farm-boy brought to safety by practice of law, intent on his mother's suffering footsteps, his inner barometer set by his bank account's weight.

Not the delicious *funtasy* of a hairy goat-man who could kick ass but also tease as though he covets mine.

Not the son I never had, providing a few years of closeness at the breast as a pupil of life, until he learned that wombs are simple bloody caverns, slots for the penile triumphant.

Yea, though I walk through the valley where longings are elixir *and* poison, I would pay any price to be free. The familiar, anguished delight of longing stymied me, in loops that drew the noose tighter. And here, as I huddle at the edge of the lake on concrete trails and picnic table grime, I pray:

If I am a fifth grader at heart, sparked by first hormones to adore the male, let this pass from me.

If I am a torn teenager with no family approval but only the option to cling to a boy, let this pass from me.

If I am the precocious college student who charms professors to sleep with her, let this pass, for I cringe before my deceptions.

If I am the trapped young wife who crosses the courtyard for sex with anyone who wears his jacket smartly, forgive me, for I am raked by loneliness.

If I ever "stole" anyone let me be certain: he was never property to be plucked and replanted, but a whirlwind of his own volition. Let me never tread on another woman's longings, for this edict will dismantle male rule: when it comes to those made in one's likeness, do no harm.

And most of all, if I am not a soul alive but an automaton driven by deep dealings of the id, may I rise from these shackles by whatever brave act I think to be beyond my ability. May I be strong enough to face the compulsion to repeat this drama: how a man pours out to a woman his whole self then begins to backtrack, a cruel reversal some say was his ruse all along. If this is the dance of damage I seek, to blindside my happiness, let it be no secret to me.

May I never give up on love, the obvious path to self-knowledge whereby essences are so thoroughly seen, recognized, and welcomed to the hearth.

A pulse beneath the deer paths I followed holds out this promise to me, under a jovial turquoise sky so inviting: *Come in! Try again!* I can but give myself only to the land erotic, or to the man shuttering his selfhood. This cheating no longer suits. I know which one has never said *never.* In the woods, I see signs, rarely kept in words, a syllabus for that special dive I make away from the house to meet the land, my faithful tonic.

23

In August of 1993, I sat at her kitchen table with Lorene. I'd been married four months to her son, an attorney she helped escape from the western plains of Kansas. She was sans one leg from diabetes, addled from a prior stroke, and when she looked at me, I wondered what she saw. But it had been a good day. She was lucid. I took the chance to ask her about Asa's birth father, Arthur Winters, because I was burning to know.

Oh, the bitterness.

"What happened in Japan? Did he ever even meet Asa?"

"Disgusting," she answered, "he was homosexual." If she was as liberal as Asa attested, she had her limits. "The drugs that went in his veins and the getting in bed with men. Yet he wanted his shirts clean and pressed in Yokohama when I was still on the maternity ward. A selfish, selfish person."

Good, I thought, *she hasn't been carrying a torch all these years.* But hatred flickered as brightly, meaning there was still attachment.

"We didn't leave Japan until Asa was a year-and-a-half. He was walking. Art wouldn't even look at him. Wouldn't touch him. Asa ran up to him, you know like kids do, wanting to play, and the man would push him away."

She went on to start the tale I already knew because Asa had studied his own case in law school and loved to tell how it startled his professor when he approached her after class: "That case you just covered? That was me."

"Years later, Art decides he wants to be a dad and comes back here," Lorene continued. "Slinking around, watching us. We fought, all the way to the state Supreme Court."

Then her mouth moved no more, but it didn't close. I waited; she was known to search and search for words that had to be the right words. I wanted to hear how she felt about the drawn-out court battle. But silence prevailed, and everything about her looked frozen.

Asa and Pops were in the next room with a baseball game on, and I yelled for them. They heaved themselves from recliners and came around the corner. "What do we do?" I pressed. The two men seemed thick with indecision.

"She told me she didn't want to be revived ever again," said Pops, and for the first time I saw that he loved her and wanted to give her this.

Asa scrambled for hope. As if this wasn't happening, as if she'd move or speak any minute. He was a kid before the inevitable grownups next lowered boom. No way was he up to being in charge. But leave her sitting at the kitchen table until she fell over? I couldn't picture how this was going to move into a close family, end-of-life-at-home moment. Asa couldn't handle that either. The men couldn't decide on a definitive course of action.

"Call an ambulance," I said.

Paramedics came and they failed. Lorene was pronounced dead on arrival at the hospital. In the coming days, picking out a casket and arranging the funeral, Asa still acted like he didn't believe it. He, Pops, and his brother moved in a fog. They'd expected it any day, but when does such a departure not stun?

Somehow, she found a way to fix it.

Asa and I headed to the visitation services at dusk. My spouse held open the door to the funeral parlor, and we cleared a small foyer. As we stepped into the room with her casket and a few seated mourners, we both saw the same thing. It lasted two seconds. And it was nothing like a horror film. It was precious and dear.

We saw Lorene sit up, look squarely in our direction, and wave to us. Turning to each other, our faces mirrored the same amazement at the same instant. The startling feature of it all, we later agreed, was her shining happiness to see us, and to be in whatever realm from where she thrust out a waving hand.

Her final stroke was not a trial for me, as I was letting go of someone I hardly knew. Asa's grief, however, was elephantine for years. It only began to wane when the babies came along. A stroke slides you too perilously close to death. Asa and I knew it, those in the stroke support-group knew it, busy professionals creating programs about stroke recovery know it. They feel death's breath at the edges of their best efforts. You have one stroke, went the lore, you'll have another someday. And the next one will kill you. It had happened to Lorene.

How could I leave Asa alone for a minute after he'd had a stroke, how could I move out?

Because he wasn't the first Daddy Man I ever had to leave.

My father had three heart-attacks, yet he was able to order Death *begone*. It worked! He lived on for decades and died of cancer instead. I grew up seeing heart attacks as deadly, but stroke seemed the more ominous partner of the vascular disasters. What smites the brain widens the ballpark where angels and demons compete—will neuroplasticity win out, or will disrepair?

But Asa and I had soothed the brain of autism—the girl was always growing and learning, if slowly and not in a linear fashion. We hadn't given up. Why give up after Asa's stroke? Pretend it's the same, I thought, just keep going.

I admired my father's strategy to put himself back together when his cardiac event demanded he change his life. He did everything he was told to do about exercise and eating right. He studied his disease fervently. After initial brooding about finality, he chose to stand up to its rule. He prevailed. I expected no less from Asa.

And because my father did not die until I was broaching midlife—despite how much he scared his children by ending up in hospitals when we were young—I shut my mind off to death and set the bar high for stroke recovery. I'd never lost someone the way the death of Asa, I knew on some level, would unhinge me.

The land and I were not one on this topic.

Rot and decay, predators on prey, vultures and others who eat the dead to sustain their own lives—these are commonplace or harrowing, smelly or ugly. That's death in organic matter, and it includes us. Repulsed by the dying process, it's easier to ignore the notion that by treating death as an equal we can live fully. We don't understand we can make peace with our eventual demise, or how that acceptance could mitigate rancor and greed.

Where is the sensuousness in death? It could be the joy of spirits passed who show themselves when you least expect it, like Lorene gleeful for one instant across the barrier between us. It happened to me again on the land.

It was another day, another walk with no purpose—I'd simply had enough of the house. Cleared for take-off and striding at a normal pace, I headed for the circle, nothing on my mind. Glancing at the back of the old barn, I was suddenly, intensely in mind of Jay-Cee, the elderly horse that joined us to become the girls' fun ride. Missing for months now, we figured she found a spot for her last rest, or that a predator took advantage of her old age. It was an open question, an enigma, and it bugged me because she'd been part of the family.

Neighbors called whenever she wandered down the road, but we'd heard from no one. She never went far anyway. She liked us. We used to let her roam the yard. We'd see her face at the bedroom window, wanting company. But she kept taking to the gravel and startling drivers, so we had to pen her in the land. She had all the acres she wanted to amble but knew her limitations and didn't venture far into the woods.

That moment on my aimless walk she invaded my mind as if she were on the trail at my side. I had a vision of her strutting, younger and lively, a beautiful brown bay with black mane, and she wanted to show me something. Pulled by her unseen lead-rope, I veered from the path and went behind the barn, noting her stall and the open door. For reasons unclear I kept walking up a small rise, pulled to it. This was the beginning ascent to Up Top, no serious climb yet, where plenty of flat spots gave opportunities to rest. I walked right to her bones. When I saw the great arches that were her ribs, the huge skull seeing sightless, the vulnerable shins picked clean but not whitened...I staggered back against a tree.

The sweet old gal knew I was worried and wanted to give me comfort. While the sudden shock of her skeleton laid out in perfect order threw me, I knew it would have been worse to find her freshly decomposing. I stayed with her fleshlessness awhile, thankful, wondering if I should take a small memento of bone for the altar. No: she'd picked this spot and she should lie here whole. I went back to the path and reached the circle, more spring in my step. I felt her circumambulating me the whole way, kicking up heels with a silent neigh.

≈

There were so many reasons to beat this stroke-thing of Asa's. His mother's stroke wasn't only about giving in. She did that later, after Pops refused to continue her therapy. He had to drive too far to take her, he said, and it wasn't doing any good. He'd canceled her health insurance just days before she had the stroke. He left her to struggle inside herself, only marshalling words among them when the midnight hour for marital contention began. She rose to that occasion but couldn't link her thoughts when Asa needed her advice.

I wasn't going to stand in the way of healing like Pops did. If anything, I was more gung-ho than the stroke victim himself.

When I stretched on the ground in the circle, thinking about loss, it was clear I didn't get the whole death thing. I clung to a belief in the longevity of strong men to protect and inspire me, even though they didn't—still not honest about this crutch that flew in the face of my feminism, this little-girl's hope.

When stroke as a life-changer strode near my aging adulthood, I felt the moorings of justice coming loose. I bargained. Asa would not die if I called his bluff by showing him that I was worth living for. I had to choose risky action to get his attention. Such was the unstated point of moving out. It was time for me to go, for both of us.

Dear Ancestors

They say you are puffs of wind now, bits of leaf, the bacteria on a badger's breath: there is no heaven, only this merger with the Earth *in vivo*. Do you come in as a mere smidge of our material world, only when it pleases you to visit?

Dead father, I have seen you in a dream, wearing a magnificent olive suit, disappearing into a wall. Are you teaching in the halls of the afterlife? Only when you stood before college students and lauded Hemingway or Poe did you reveal the real man, woven with the things you saw in the great minds that pulled you into the self where truth is. That thing you always did, once you were Dad and no longer Daddy: you sat on the couch, checked out from your surroundings, and reviewed the day's several humiliations. You withdrew into literary critique for a hit of fuel to handle the world always out to stifle you, anger you, prevent you from filling a room with your presence.

You learned to fill it with your absence instead. Asa noticed this at his bachelor party, where you did the same thing: "uncanny—like he wasn't even there. But clearly there he sat." Couldn't you have found a way to spark the slow and beer-soaked conversations for one night? Couldn't you have hunkered down for me?

My deceased brother, you were dead to life long before C. Difficile took you down. You took on the bodhisattva role among the mentally ill. You were the one who always wanted to help were it not for the iron sleep caused by your prescriptions and the ward dramatics of your institutionalized girlfriend.

My big brother was brought low. As he adapted to halfway houses and nursing homes, he forgot how to spin delicate theorems, traverse the byways of chaos theory, and forgot, in short order, the atomic structures that adorn the periodic table.

You couldn't work as a chemist in the rat race, so you let chemistry work you over, via clinical trials and the eighteen-hour naps. Some designate the disabled as useless and hand them a career of stupor until their lives are over, like you. Were you only biding time, Brother? Do you now spend your days in the afterlife, in wild research beyond the grasp of us dullards—so exhilarating you are too busy to speak to me through a reputable medium?

My grandmother—not the dear, sad one but the other one— remember how I drove you to the church confessional so you could release your resentments? You never tried very hard with me, though I came to stay frequently, as a visitor from the suburbs. You had closer-by and less confusing grandkids to offer your wry smiles. I was your only daughter's only daughter, chain links whose importance you never examined. You told me I had broad shoulders; I asked if that was a bad thing; *Well,* you answered pityingly, *football players have broad shoulders.* So young and you saw right through me: malformed! Not girl enough!

But I kept trying. I listened to your recriminations against the great aunts, I watched your thin, humped back, your arms crossed as we struggled to be companions, as you went on in bitterness that dipped to self-deprecation so fast I couldn't wait to jump on a horse's back and get to the pasture. Have you fixed yourself in the other world yet? Have you learned to forgive yourself for teaching my mother her critical aim that put me in her sights whenever I opened my mouth?

These three never saw me. None I can call saint. You all haunt my thoughts; if you're looking on, do I interest you now? I struggle to attribute grace to your censored lives and difficult deaths. I don't want to end up as you lived, or how you died. So go on, be the rustling leaves, be the rain. Don't tread on this, my reverie in the arms of now: something the three of you, so bent on logging others' crimes, rarely came to taste.

Dear ancestors, the land keeps healing this old heart. Unlike a fountain of youth, the land erotic is God in perpetual cogitation of beauty. I may judge lopsidedly your deaths but will not wear a single edict from one of them. I will run, but I will keep looking back, with a purpose. Death isn't putting Asa under its thumb, but the death of my daily presence may be the ticket to make him choose life.

24

Talking to the land was different once I decided to pack my things for departure.

I knew I'd be back periodically, for that was the arrangement: there was no way I'd give up time with our daughters. Sierra wanted to stay with dad. Nina already had some nights away, initially in a group home when her school lobbied for it, and later at a caregiver's. We would all meet up at our house on Wednesdays and weekends. For the rest of it, I'd become a townie again.

"How can I leave you?" I asked the land. "Will you feel differently about me?" I spun with emotions confused by the lack of a clear future. I didn't know with what eyes to view the place. I anthropomorphized it in the worst way, waiting for a blessing to pack with my belongings. And I remembered everything, and in person, on a last walk before I walked out.

The sprawling backyard was laden with memories of daughters in kiddie swimming pools, the black locust trees leaning over such revelry. I remembered the way we'd inhabit that yard, eating watermelon and watching the chickens go gluttonous over discarded rinds. On darkest nights, we huddled around the fire pit I dug alone one afternoon in a rush of adrenalin, where backyard slips into farmyard—if you could call it that. The animals were long gone now.

The animal lover in Asa died with his stroke. We once adopted a gaggle of five geese, not tame enough to pet, but bonded to us. That is, after they rushed off the minute they arrived—charging the length of the driveway, flying down the road to where the creek is roofed by a cement bridge. "Write when you get work!" Asa called wistfully. The geese proceeded to look about, look at us, then waddle back to the house. From then on, until predators picked them off, they were the watchdogs we counted on, dropping splatters of poop but raising a ruckus over guests or intruders, responding in cacophony when Asa walked to his car yelling, "Goo-sters!" It was Asa who locked them into their little house for safety every night. Now I couldn't bear the sight of their hut still standing, weeds eyehigh in the pen, fence wire flexing loose on sagging posts.

The chicken house Asa built—larger, impressive—stood empty, too. One-hundred-and-fifty hens rolled out eggs to wash and tote to the health food store to make a buck—the charm collapsing when two human infants arrived in quick succession. The coop sits with its floor composting next to the faded barn, also a relic of the vibrant Asa in his workshop—tools still hanging there on neat pegboard, rusting. Why put myself through this, a last look devoid of solace or insight?

Beyond the gate is the land I fear to tread. I've turned this once-exalted mystery school and scene of sexually spirited vision into a Lyme incubator now. I go more often to parks or asphalt walkways. It's come to that.

The path to my circle winds two mower-widths wide, and ticks be damned, I needed a look before I cut ties. One subtle curve then another before the wild. In the beginning the walk was flanked solely by meadow and two slight trees. After a few years, the fledgling elms and hedge got out of hand, and we had a big snipper-tractor cut them down. I was nostalgic for the openness, the way things used to be. I thought if I could restore the open meadow, I could restore the openness in my husband's heart. Those were the days he was traveling, traveling, working, working, shut down except to father the youngest. His clients' dramas were his hobby then.

One walnut tree alerts me to the circle ahead. Two-trunked, as are many of the trees on the land, it reminds of the cutting done by the former owners—and a blunder of mine years ago. When a city boyfriend and I were freezing in a rented farmhouse and he couldn't tell tree from tree, I picked *Juglans nigra* wrongly, guessing it was an ash tree that would burn green. I condemned a walnut to the chainsaw instead. Beautiful dark-grained thing, no matter how many I have planted to make up for that, I still mourn.

At the edge of the circle an Osage orange trails a weeping drape. There's a section nearby that I mowed for a time, as if it would be a campground someday. But canes of wild rose took over, surrounding a baby oak that stands, a skinny sentry on watch. No matter how Asa and I dreamed of "sharing the land," we chose to close ourselves off within it.

Once a serving of furniture is carted into town and declared mine, I know I'll never again be the same in the circle. The upcoming shift in family life made me barge one last time into deeper woods. Farther in I'm less conspicuous, less the point, less defined by where home stands.

Back here is something that sends me, watcher and old friend, a message that *you are still peripheral.* Not because I'm vile or stupid, but because of what I can't see or know. Especially at night when I rarely ever come, feeling like an intruder and a little scared.

Why did I never camp in the woods at night? It felt like there were things I shouldn't see. I also wonder if it's because of the rumors of mountain lions in the area, or because timber rattlers slither at night. More courageous naturalists might forge in, but I don't want to push my luck with other species, don't want to make them hurt me because I stepped wrong. On top of it all, it's simply sad to feel utterly defeated by the tiny tick.

Even before Lyme, I thought the land itself wanted me to vacate whenever the sunset's show was over. In deepest dusk I could sense it saying *go on, go now*. A plea for privacy because things are going to shift. A real shaman would be invited to stay.

In the center of these acres is the mottled sycamore who spoke about forgiveness. Why can't I luck into another teaching? Because I've already made up my mind. As wisdom purveyors, the trees are closed for business. Nearby the creek spreads and makes shallows, rarely wet unless a torrent pours for days. The rocks are patient old timers sitting on the front porch of my awareness. I simply walk up the dry creek then, to what I named, in earlier and more optimistic days, the Earth Healing Circle. Only a stone's throw from the grandfather tree I put in charge of the four spirits who didn't get to come womb-ward.

It's so overgrown. The land has reverted to the buckbrush I cut back, an underground community humored by the swinging scythe. Here is where the property line comes off the neighboring hill and begins its ascent to the back edge. I once made a trail along the barbed wire fence because I wanted to think about ownership occasionally. The edge of the lover's body, distinct from the sheets.

Over yonder, someone else can shoot guns. That's the language spoken in the distance on rare occasions, pops and booms, trigger fingers unseen, never a hiker or a practical woodsman, no neighbor with or without deer trails to follow and a need to pray.

This is how I believe that as far as I can see is mine to love, whether it says so on paper or not.

I thought if I were going to conjure the walker in the woods who loved me in fantasy so arousing it felt real, it would be here. But how can I lust now? Sorrow and anticipation hold the cards. I sit on a lump of lichen-spotted limestone anyway and wait.

There is an image in my mind before a leaf rustles. He is here. Down there! In the dry creek bed, on the next-door whoever's land. He looks not himself.

So that's it—satyrs age too! Horny, flippy, kick-up-your-heels priapic teasers get the slowdowns like me. His hair is white now, like mine in a narrow edging from crown to ear. His step is less than lithe. He's picking his way over the rocks; doesn't he sense me? With that thought, he turns, just as he did the first time, slowly, and with a piercing eye: *I have always seen you. For the one you are when you are here, body and soul. I couldn't care less about what you do in the crosshairs of obligation. Nor did I tell you I wouldn't get old along with thee. Wanna check me out for old time's sake? How about a little spin on this?* And again, his member rises. He has no hormonal issues. He doesn't need the drugs. Nor a loincloth. We can do it with the distance between us, all I need do is spread my legs and that will signal *begin.*

But he's an old guy, and I'm ashamed that I liked him better young. I simply sit where I am, frozen, legs crossed, a look that says *I'm sorry, I'm sorry, I'm sorry for everything. Even your loss.*

He reads the rejection with no ruefulness or regret. But suddenly I know where he is going. He's leaving my land because I am, too, and because I haven't worked out my angst about aging, and because it's harder to get wet these days, young man or otherwise. He'll travel until winter, avoiding the buttoned-up homes, very careful about women alone in the woods. Respectful. Understanding that he limps, he's gotten thick around the middle, fronds at the base of his penis are white and his balls are bare. One day, he will lie down in the snow and not get up.

But no. The set of his shoulders as he moves out of sight tells me I'm wrong. Maybe he won't be the one getting up or getting it up, but he will compost. He will sink white hair, old bones and limp genitalia into the leaf mold that is thick in an oak and hickory forest, and he will be erased by frost, blizzard, and the merciless wind that ices branches then leaves them to drip.

But another will rise. His successor will be schooled by how the seasons fold over into newness from death. This one will also wear the exact features from the land that births him when no one is looking—not even a doe, a deer, a female deer.

Until someone no stranger to the land erotic stalks him, he will not age. I picture her, inquisitive. Then if life breaks her, he will bear the burden, but he will bear it as the Man O' The Woods, and she should never stop believing, the way I did.

Lonelier than ever, I head Up Top.

Now for the moment of ambivalence that turns on a dime into wonder: the cedars that reach and spread into Deer Nation grew more formidable as the years flew by. I feel the same reticence as with the night woods: *don't go in.* They have trampled their kingdom of any weed underfoot to accommodate pristine needle flooring. It's eerie and otherworldly, but there is no sign of them. My senses clutch around a fear of Lyme.

The back fence borders a different reality: open pasture coats the other side and nameless humans deploy cattle that keep it free of stalk or stem. A bevy of black heifers roam so far from any house that they find my appearance interesting. After the sobering departure of the Wood Man, they are fun to watch. They're on alert because predators usually come out of the woods, but still, I could be one of those people who bring them salt-blocks and hay. "Carry on!" I call, and don't look back.

This is the back route to the top of the land. Cedars and other hardwoods took over, making it tricky to find open space—we never contracted to bring the big snipper thing up here. But at last, the land's third and most remote circle, one that I swear I like best of all when I make the effort to be here, emerges. I can't find the holey rocks I laid out to mark the center. Here is where ownership is a wan joke because sky is the ruler to whom I pay homage. Up Top.

I used to inventory the possibilities. Asa and I would build a log-cabin lean-to at the edge of this circle. We'd construct a house up here, leaving the one below for office space. Grow our own feed for poultry, sheep, and pigs. Thin the cedars and fill the ravine that was deepening yearly. Manage the woods entire, every thoughtful cut a mercy killing.

Instead, we abandoned this back-forty, and I learned not to dream at its expense.

The tour is closed. The sights will shift and spread in their urge for each day to be unique, but likely unseen by human eyes. One daughter is on sensory overload nonstop and needs familiar rooms and faces only. The other, obsessed with her peer group and garnering accolades at school, is no longer a roamer, looking at her land just for the looks of it. And Asa? He will never gather the stamina to make it Up Top again.

How do you separate husband and place, when we started out co-owners of a new beginning, when I cheated on him by loving it more? It became the real marriage, and I couldn't tell him? For Asa, the land was a buffer from other people. Not a teeming populace he wanted to get personal with, not mystery, not even relaxing enough to wander.

When he pulled away from us both, I partnered with the land. So many trees. But trees don't rip out their roots and walk up to a man, collar him, and warn him to do better. The land told me long ago that justice is often slower than water carving a rock.

Owls sound off in every season down the hollow between our house and the neighbor's easement. Owl of wisdom or owl of death? The symbolism is mixed, but either way a harbinger of change. To their chorus I ended my last walk as resident student, gathering up influences for the next landscape that would hold me close.

Darkness Anyway

I pull the strength of the quiet around me. I ask that my ancestors, upbraided or unfathomable, stand against bad dreams. For I cobbled together some courage to come to the circle and spend the night's currency into dawn.

I ask that the spouse sleeping in the house gently submerge under the gauze that MaryJane gives him; may no anxious scenes protrude until he rises. It's too late for music or awareness—the needs of his clients consume the brain that blood flow forsook. The whirr of the sleep apnea machine erases dialogue and docket calls for now.

For me, facing down fear won't be a lark.

But I'll stay here and suffer the night. Right now, rigid in sitting posture by a fire out in the open, knees drawn up, knobby placeholders for my chin, there's but one thing I wish to convey: spirits, I am no threat. I simply want to see how you cavort, how you coagulate without me (*please, don't mind me!*), how you let loose the creatures and at what moment bathe the verdancy with dew. Drown me then, too.

But you know I want more. I want to assuage the utter terror of a future without home, I want your blessing, I want a big fat reassurance that all will be well. I want too much. Have I ever been less than greedy in your bosom?

Osage, buckbrush, hickory, and burr oak, lean into me. I'll sleep in the mummy-tight satchel of a sleeping bag as if its synthetic touch bestows safety. I'll leave my head poked out for the sacred. To the land erotic I beseech: play me with sounds I can't name, and you may give me the sense of being stared at, if you must. I will curl about these low flames and call it romance, for fear is not our way.

If you will have me, my night-shift proprietor, despite what I said about never trespassing your secrets, here I am in darkness anyway.

25

I dreamed of a city-nest with wood floors and light-streaming glass, waking to quiet and my own time. Driving by houses or small apartment complexes with "For Rent" signs, the obsession was entirely private. I was searching for rooms that would match what was going on inside me. Impossible to say exactly what that was—other than the sense of siege—but I wanted to find out.

Many apartments were inspected, and I determined not to settle for a hovel out of shame. For it was right to make this move. I could no longer subject my daughters to their parents stomping furiously on eggshells. I'd given up asking Asa, "Why do you hate me so?" It prevented the reply that invariably blamed the stroke.

We fell into each day like opponents running for the same office, trading offense for defense. My position: exhortations to health (and to reason), pressing harder the more I was ignored, making me a shrill sound in Asa's ears. Mostly I defended my pride, so easily injured, and my sanity loosened from its moorings as The Four Horsemen drew Asa into realms more paranoid and defensive about his short-term memory loss.

Whither compassion? Forgiveness? I identified with deer on my county roads at night when the lights bear down, forgetting legs and instinct as the machine approaches—louder, closer. Asa could be all-encompassing with his anger, scorn, and withdrawal. Yet I knew he needed something. Something I *did* want to give if I could pin down what it was. He wasn't in the mood to clarify, and I failed at turning the other cheek. I couldn't release Daddy Man to a personality change that, whether he cared, may have become a biological fact.

Then the place was found, auspiciously near Sierra's high school. Besides being my retreat, the duplex-apartment would function as a haven for her. The space was decidedly vintage— kitchen, bathroom, and bedrooms were humble cubicles with blemishes and drafts—but wood floors spanned a spacious living and dining area that held the morning and afternoon sun. In the front yard grew the three tallest oak trees on the block. A pair of lofty sycamores stood across the street, echoes of the land I'd no longer greet daily.

I was up for the town experience though, where the wild is patronized in parks. A human way with color and pattern make up for the artifice. I became mad about parks. Nature fleshes out the contours of community in such spaces. Parks exhibit a cultivated deliberation with little input except from the sky in the form of re-portable weather. It had been years since I was able to people-watch, and I approached my opportunities in earnest.

In the apartment I had space and quiet, but little to fill it. The placing of my two armchairs, desk, and some waterfowl prints only emphasized the theme: sparse. For a bed, a camping air mattress. Asa was less than thrilled with helping me drag stuff from our home.

It was late when I finally moved the last of my things. Nina was at a caregiver's overnight; I'd deliberately shielded her from seeing the severance in progress. She calmly received the fact that mom was getting an apartment, and she'd come see me there sometimes. Sierra was upstairs refusing to watch me walk out of our house. Sierra was tough, I told myself, for she'd never shown a wobble of dismay about her parents' discord. I told her I was leaving, and her grunt was nonchalant. "I'll see you over there tomorrow," I yelled up the stairs, trying to weave threads of continuity she could hold onto.

The hard facts were that Nina was used to her father's lack of attention, and Sierra fiercely sided with him and shut me out. She was furious, but there was no reconciliation in the offing. I lost my privileges to the inside of her heart when I lost the energy to be gentle, and she offered me a way out of trying harder. Her tough demeanor and disgust with me made the story a useful salve: the strong Sierra. In my depleted state I chose to believe it and minimize my role in her barricaded posture. Whenever I tried to discuss it, she said, "I'm hoping for divorce, myself!" Her eyes were livid, and I was crushed.

I left Asa in his recliner, not knowing what to make of his face and too worn down to care. It was a new face, an off-guard face, as if he didn't know what to think, say, or believe. I turned away before a waft of guilt hit me. He would be okay. If only he would sit there and think about what he did to bring this moment about! I didn't linger at the threshold because I needed to rush past my own feelings. I knew this wasn't an authentic goodbye. It was, on the generous side, a cry for help that Asa was too overwhelmed to rise to, but I wouldn't admit that. It was, on the judgmental side, an attempt to teach a lesson while taking pains to keep appearances intact. I'd be back again and again. I was hardly dreaming about divorce. Just about running.

But the first night in my apartment was a holy heart-wrenching hell. The ceiling was too high, the closet too tall. My camping mattress rose only inches from the wood floor. The landlady had a sonar device that repelled rodents and insects, so I tried to feel privileged: I'd never have dared this at home, where it was difficult to keep mice from partying among their hangouts in the wee hours. There the cats had plenty to do but here: no pets. I was grateful for that—no one else to look after. I scrambled to come up with some pluses to steady my nerves.

Sleep wouldn't be wrapped by darkness as on the land. A back porch light shone in, and a main road artery beamed as traffic swooshed. Despite blackout curtains, I was aware of the house next door where beefy college boys sat among tiki torches. My little cell wasn't home.

I heard female voices match the guffaws from the patio next door and thought to myself, *you've really done it now. You severed yourself from everything you love, including the land. Tell me, once more, why?*

Because I need to breathe and be assured of life. I had to hop off the Damn-the-Torpedoes-to-Death train that Asa rode daily.

Terror didn't dissolve in that foreign room with my bumpy airbed. I'd had no time to hang a picture on the wall or drag in end tables I couldn't reach from the floor anyway. The anguish built and I had a date with it: either meet the moment or call it a mistake. But this new chapter had been an ordeal to set up. Asa gave me a small stipend to help pay the rent in exchange for my continuing to work in the law office on weekends. To renege now was no option, especially since I believed I would endure this night, eventually sleep, agree to carry on into a future that was blank but for the continuing necessity that mandated separation.

Asa never really resisted the idea. I was a weight on his life. He barely squelched anger while helping me move, but he did it. The only sign of regret I saw was that unarranged face in the last instant as I walked out. He could have said, "Don't!" Or even, "I don't like this," or tried to insult me or *something*. But nothing, except that look: like a little boy nervous on the first day of kindergarten who wasn't sure his mom would pick him up when it was over. Like a man who wished it hadn't gone all wrong.

26

I read books, went to my job, and hosted both daughters as they tried to make sense of adolescence. I wrote in a journal to hear myself think. And I walked.

I told myself I walked to figure things out, but did no such thing, propelled through the streets of the older neighborhood I now called mine. The blocks of homes set side-by-side had an *I am what I am* kind of feel, with neither the flourish of the historical section nor the harrumph of the higher-priced set. I liked the area, though. There were some plain little boxes, but most houses sported bygone style and plucky renovations.

I sat on my tiny front porch or traversed the safe streets, an initiate into urban Eros. Two decades of creek and wild acres erupted into a hunger for the human swirl. I could feel them inside their houses; I stared as they opened garages and slowly backed out driveways. Strangers walked by or rode bikes down the middle of the street—I felt related to anyone who crossed my path when I was at the duplex. I took them into my mind as fellow sufferers, undoubtedly with their own poignant stories to tell. Urban Eros, my people.

I was especially fond of my own block and couldn't get over the warmth I felt when my feet regained its confines after a trek. I lived near my workplace and went to use the high school's stadium track like many neighborhood people did after hours. There was such a satisfaction being among them, knowing we were drawn together to this circle of fake grass and smelly rubber beneath our feet—intimates, these locals and I marching the course to lose a few pounds. I sighed contentedly at the seamlessness between work and neighborhood as it must have been in the old days. In my loneliness, it was cozy: eros not as wild sex but a daily stew of connection.

A single man rented a small house across the street, and I nursed a fantasy for a pleasant break in my misery. I saw him watching me through his screen door a time or two, a curiosity kiboshed when Asa and kids came over. I couldn't determine his age so decided it was acceptable. On summer nights I glimpsed him through partially open windows while I sat on my porch in the dark, staring down all the trouble I could get into. But I was dried up and closed shut. Or was I? While still working on the courage to say hello, a semi-sized moving van backed into his narrow driveway and the next morning he was gone.

Desire to scrutinize the houses on block after block continued. Pulled by brisk strides, I peered past yards to the doors and rooflines, head swiveling to scan the opposite side of the street. House exteriors somehow a tell who has sunk roots there and how they lived. Would I ever be as happy as they were? I wasn't just placing me in the houses to try on a fit. I put my whole family inside and saw us transformed.

As if a new house would do it! I walked these streets dreaming awake. Sometimes I gave Asa a man-cave and bigger television, and in this daydream he was so grateful that he used it judiciously and came out of himself to join us more often. The girls gushed over being in town instead of isolated in the country, with friends on the block plus every electronic device that teenagers could want. The furniture was fresh and comfortable, the energy uses efficient. These material things were symbols, not literal consumer urges: reverie spun around the happiness of my family. I gave them everything they wanted, and at last they loved me and loved their lives and that was enough.

In the newness of marital separation any pleasure sparked by the opposite sex feels illicit. After nightfall when I could no longer walk about the neighborhood, I read. The first book gave me a safe thrill. Admiring the author from afar was all I could do.

An admirer of Thomas Moore, I sat in my lonely apartment and settled down to *The Re-enchantment of Everyday Life.* Here's where readers get to know the man, his views on everything from furniture to sports, each topic a warm but stimulating massage on art, theology, sex, or politics. How someone could be so brimming with opinions and deliver them with such gentle largesse is the essence of his mastery.

Moore's viewpoint as a former monk who chose marriage and family is sexy for starters. As my first book in the new place, I welcomed the author like a handsome friend, open but not overbearing. He got me through some lonely hours. What is it about Moore's wording that is erudite, spiritual, friendly, challenging, and comforting at the same time? It goes beyond *style*. I avoid celebrities and doubt that Moore acts like one, but the guy consistently hits the bestseller list.

I fell gratefully into *The Soul of Sex* when I had an inkling my body could return from vaginal atrophy and dry nipples. I trusted Thomas Moore to guide me, but as usual his magic was indirect. Here's a man smitten by his own preferred Greek figure, the winsome Aphrodite. He has examined her every nuance. She speaks to him; perhaps he has seen Venus statues blink but isn't telling.

What a relief to read a man totally devoid of the usual penis-goaded rush, or the tantalizing fear of a grand seductress. He relates to her and doesn't idolize or objectify her, maybe because she shows him how to connect sexually to self and others.

I came across *The Soul's Religion* next. The cover did a lot for me. Moore perches by water's edge that matches his clothing in green and brown earth-tones, and he's grinning like he's found the best seat in the house. Sitting in and among the waterweeds on the bank like he grew out of them, as if he belonged to them. I know the feeling.

Moore is no satyr trailing a come-hither scent through sensuous wordplay, careful just often enough to remind us of the wife. But I could imagine him walking in the woods with the urgency of the stag in his eyes. How do I know this?

His cover photograph for this collection of essays, his face in the water's reflection: you must turn the book upside down to see. It's him but not him. There can be no doubt he approved such a public statement about the generous portion of pagan purity in his soul.

Dear Streets

Newly found arteries, holy grid of everything I should hate, give me your tar and your potholes, your wispy blown trash and roaring vehicles. I have sidewalks, and as a pedestrian, faith in being seen as one who will yield. A vulnerable walker, I don't keep my head down but neither do I smile. I'm not afraid of the street's pace, not because of danger-thrill but as one drunk with the traveler's opened eye. I must be in love with your toxins, your unclean aggregates awash in bitumen—sly devils are the men of oil and gas, using the same dirty grease to lay down a go-way to make cars' exploding engines faster still. Petroleum is a mighty clan: its smell overpowers and turns my stomach like a bad boy that promises excitement.

Dear streets, you might as well be new to me.

I had been living "in the country." Roads are gravel and packed earth, narrow, not for the jogger. We of the country drive everywhere and consider our chariots part of the collateral damage to the land, a strangely justified injury so that we may pay homage. We only unsheathe the practical eye in town, where we come to get our staples and amusements. Our wheel wells hold more than mud: they hold the particulate of our beloved place, although to "Sunday drivers" it's our sorry sully. We drop the dust and ochre splatters onto the floors of drive-through washes quickly. We are not of the urban world, and we will leave it, to grow muddy again, gobs and streaks worn on our car doors like a badge. We are landed gentry in our minds; redneck commuters to town dwellers.

Except. Land baroness no more, I was back to dear streets, forsaken since I was a child pushing the edges of the neighborhood or a drunk teenager walking home to sober up. I acclimate myself to the city—as an "older woman" unleashed.

However. In honor of the cultural obsession with the automobile, I talk to my vehicle. It has sadly worn gray upholstery, and the nearly visible energy imprints of kid car seats and grocery sacks. The scum in the cup holders won't yield to cleaning. I tell it, *even now as your huff and hum quiets into a rented garage, the land quixotic waits attentive as a dog before the picture window for when its owner draws from inaudible to nearby.*

Dear streets, current aphrodisiac—I still know where I belong.

27

Asa and I continued our relationship from two residences. When I was at the house, we slept in the same bed, clinging but silent, occasionally attempting sex. We parented our children, spent holidays together, went out to eat and fought about money. He was still distant and contemptuous, but now I could get away. I thought he'd accepted the arrangement as the new norm. Briefly, he saw a personal trainer and a physical transformation began that brought back the sparkle in his eye and some affection for me. I thought we were on our way to a slow rebirth.

But on Valentine's Day, someone else fell into his lap.

≈

I adored the dark, subterranean sushi café with its elevated tables where customers sat on cushions, shoes removed, behind curtains. I was pleased that Asa asked me out. We ended up at a tiny table near the bar, shoved against an aquarium.

There was a release about him, a lighter mood. We talked about our daughters and daily stuff until the food came.

"We should look at where we're at. You and me," he began. Not businesslike, but breezy.

"Finally!" I leaned in. "We never talk about it. My move. Our marriage."

"We need to face facts."

"Like . . . ?"

"Like it's been three months. You're obviously not coming home. I think I need to move on."

My fork hung in mid-air. That moment where you know what's coming but you hope it won't ruin the moment: I was aware of the silver tines and how the food was about to turn to ash.

"Let me get this straight. We've been acting like married people but some nights I sleep alone in town. We do everything together, keeping it normal for the kids. We've never talked about what's going on, so without any discussion, you're just saying we're done?"

"May I remind you? You. Moved. Out."

"But the natural order of things . . ." I paused. ". . . would be to talk about the last few months! What's going on?"

Asa looked so at ease. Attractive. His mood was jaunty.

I put the fork down. "Oh my god, no."

"I might want to date somebody."

"Since when?"

"It just happened."

"Who?" That was all I could manage.

"I don't think you ever met her. She hasn't been a client for a while. Her daughter is T. G."

I'd typed more motions and journal entries for that case than I cared to remember.

"Wait. Isn't her mom, your new paramour, highly involved with the case as the grandmother providing childcare? And do T. G. and the kid still live with her?"

His reply was too fast: "Doesn't matter, she's not my client."

"You son of a bitch," I whispered.

"*You* moved out."

My husband looked at his plate, a long history with seafood a pleasure never diminished and hardly forsaken now. He dug in.

On the curb as Asa drove off from the deadly date, I stood like a refugee: where do I go now? What do I do? His manner was astoundingly akin to someone who did not care about me one micro-bit. But I knew why. He didn't see me. He was falling for love itself.

≈

Psychology: Jealousy is a loss. You hate the rival with all your heart. What's wrong with me, you ask? I *knew* I was so bad that my lover would eventually be repelled.

Biology: Wake up! There's a threat to the couple or family unit here. Jealousy is a sign that you must overcome the rival and keep everyone together.

Feminism: Jealous men get angry, respond with violence. Jealous women internalize and feel despair. A man worries more about his partner's sex act with another. A woman feels stabbed because the container of intimacy and relationship is broken.

Anarchism: Jealousy occurs when partners foolishly assume property rights over each other. That's capitalism. Property is theft, so the partner becomes an owned object. The relationship is not egalitarian.

Religion: The couple unit is God-ordained. Forgive the transgression and stay together.

I wish any of these angles meant a damn when a desperate woman's eye wandered in Asa's direction. Every one of them fits somehow. The urge to settle on a root explanation is exhausting—

I'm weak before the green-eyed monster, always have been. When Asa answered the woman's interest, I never should have hounded her on Facebook, sleuthed out her address, or sent angry poems about her Destroyer aspect. I went to a therapist, unable to sleep. The therapist chided me for "boundary invasion."

It's easy to shame jealous persons, recipients of torture with a universal twist. This realm of hell for them is like when the beloved dies a physical death, but eerily, he still walks. What if there is a *different body* that jealousy hurts most of all?

We can talk about emotions as the site of injury and let it go at that. I tended to suffer to the point of insanity when betrayed by sexual means. But what about the other envelope, the body around the body, the one with all the colors?

Search *human energy field* and marvel at the images. Some come from a type of photography that purports to capture the subtle body. Some cite ancient yogic texts that place seven energy centers at physiological junctures, whirling vortexes that correspond to human emotion and perception.

If you look at these beautiful images, and only the most dulled and skeptical eye would not, you will note how the self-contained energy field outlines the individual. Another body entirely cocooning the one that's flesh and blood.

Reiki, a way of healing that seeks to manipulate this field to ease all manner of ailments, is the people's choice for how to touch such a body. Therapeutic touch is a favorite in hospitals. Yet little is said about what happens when braided energies get torn. How do we fare when subtle bodies accustomed to traveling in tandem are blasted apart with a poor prognosis for repair?

When couples split, the aura may turn gray. But what happens to the environment around the bond when demolition happens in earnest?

I wonder what hue jealousy makes, this menace that can encompass and derail me. Did we just decide to call envy a putrid-green because jealousy nauseates? Is the injury of jealousy a unique color, or the same shade as overall trauma? Where and how does this loss show in the shifting rainbow made by the unseen energy-bodies connected, beloved to beloved? All I felt was that choking gray.

Sexual betrayal is a whopper of a disruption. Maybe the sexual nature has its own energetic signature and spin? Or is my imagination playing with color and motion to avoid the real feelings of knife in the belly, scream at the ready?

Aura-talk speaks of the fields getting "dirty." Jealousy made the very essence of me feel rubbed out with a used eraser. When people assert that sexual betrayal hurts like no other pain, they know that the burden is a life event. But what's the diameter of the pain? It is as wide as fibers stretching from a country house to a duplex in town.

"You moved out!" It was Asa's answer to every problem posed. For the person left behind, the move-out is the ultimate indignity. They don't understand how to read drastic measures as the cry for help. The mover's farewell imparts a free pass to all forms of retaliation and disregard. For Asa, romancing a former client was not an affair, simply the next and entitled step of his journey.

I understand why he had an extra helping of outrage. As a young husband married to his high-school sweetheart, he came home one day to an entirely empty house. She had taken every stick of furniture and booked it. Never did he forgive, never did the bitterness abate. I had to handle this bundle of dynamite gingerly our entire relationship, that and every other loss in Asa's life, especially Lorene. His energy-body brimmed with memories that stoked the bed of coals beneath his fear of abandonment. The Borderline's curse!

Every day post-sushi-date that my beloved lusted for his former client was an agony to wake to. I had to walk at the lake non-stop or throughout the neighborhood until it was pitch dark and time for bed, or I wouldn't get a few hours' sleep. I could only stem the panic outdoors. I returned to the duplex apartment after a generous slice of free time with plant life and sky in the fully open air. I needed it like medicine.

Jealous thoughts jump to conclusions: *he's going to move her in, marry her, I will lose my kids. I will lose my land. Well, maybe I want to! I can't bear this, and it's a reminder of what went wrong. We can't fix it.*

I always did gauge my right mind or lack of it by how cut off I felt from the land. Because, of course, despite that tremulous last walk and a night in the circle where there were no visions nor answers—only forbearance—we continued, my land and me. Despite my move, despite Lyme. Nothing changed in our bond. But not every day is bliss out there, an instant *ahhhh*. Some walks I was a robot going through the motions, lamenting *this is not fair, I deserve to connect with the Mystery!* It can take an hour or so for the soul to come out of hiding. Or not.

But jealousy of another woman setting foot on the land? I was willing to throw away the real marriage if it meant I could gain a permanent end to the hell-marriage to Asa.

In three weeks, she dumped him.

Just that quickly, for me greeting the day became an easier proposition, but things were never the same. On family nights at our house, I started to sleep on the couch and never with Asa, sorry for the daughters to see this. Divorce was imminent, and on top of it I entertained the idea of severance from the land forever. I could go anywhere! But the thought of another locale loomed like a trip to an alien planet.

Asa made a point of telling me how he berated the woman up one side and down the other the night she told him they were through. Words among *them*! I was glad in the meanest sort of way.

Then I went to the back edge of the deer's hideout, Up Top and back along the creek to tell the whole place that I was sorry. I realized there had never been any hard feelings. The land was the same, the welcome was the same. I was grateful that this was my gift for losing my mind to jealousy. The land was good, either way—go or stay. It didn't pout or demand allegiance.

When we anthropomorphize, sometimes it's childish what we come up with. On the other hand, were there subtle bodies on those acres that I loved these twenty years? I may have been a human with bad pictures in my head, but can I be certain that I was the only species out there at creekside, or under the dome of an oak, who felt pain about the affair and its aftermath?

28

For the first time ever, the circle of stones didn't dislodge the needles of anxiety that poked in one place then another, refusing to give their real names. The circle asked me to look at what jealousy brought to pass. I had bundled in layers for the tail end of winter and lay prone on frozen ground to drink the light that heals, on a stark March noon. At times, the wind moved so forcefully that it threw moving pictures on the sky that were made of clouds and the bare branches below—furiously waving—couldn't eclipse the show overhead. Clouds advanced and streamed away, wind running me through with softness, penetrating the synthetic layers I wrapped in and making a slit over my heart and my sex— dropping in sensations I can't figure out.

Am I taken by these clouds racing oddly low, or I am the taker, pulling in their forcefulness before they scoot out of sight, trying in to recover from recent events? *Conquer the ancient fear*—is that their message? Neither cumulus formations nor pretty wisps, they don't look like a man or stand for any shape. Blobs on the run—they refuse to anthropomorphize. They shift, rend, and stretch over me, bumping one another to the blue backdrop. There is plenty of sky between their temporary bodies thin to the light. I will lie down for this as long as I can, rigid with a fear that doesn't seem fair.

I can't rule out that the wind is trying to be my lover as it propels these clouds free for the watching. If this be the wind's art of love then please, I ask, let the fear be fucked out of me. I give you—close clouds, sweeping gusts—my body in missionary position on this bed of cold ground that you skim low and speed across to others who will be touched and cry out, until somewhere the wind is spent and "dies." Notice how often it dies after nightfall, not one to quit of a sudden.

Is this the only way I can think about power: who's doing the ravishing? Seems like anthropomorphizing of the most limiting kind. I wish I could see the wind as power without purpose aimed anywhere and participate in wind for wind's sake, which just happens to be barreling over my body.

There is such an urge to scour the erotic from this experience: I'm cold, my coat's too tight, the ground is inflexible, and, although the pain ended when the client rejected Asa, I bear the knowledge of his lust for another woman. My aura's still blackened before these clouds that are nothing but pure.

Jealousy should be past tense already, never to be spoken of again. I could simply admire clouds streaming overhead. Laud power as the pinnacle of the Nature experience. Hide in narrative, break down power into acceptable forms of aesthetic embrace. Plunder the laden table of metaphor by drafting nature into sonnets that specify the borders of joy and forget about petty human stuff. Anything not to be a fool with a fetish, right? Cloud fetish, water fetish, bare-ground fetish. What is it I really want? Sex with the wind? Or to worship past the human condition, to tame it?

In every addiction there is the lust for God, especially in the likes of Mother Earth as a nurturing all-womb. Especially if I allow that—as a sticker on my youngest's phone attests—*All monsters are human.* So, we sanctify the crystal meth, the shopping, the sweet ice cream, the hook-up you close your eyes to when you come and scream a holy name. If these pleasures were not the closest you could come to God, wouldn't you resist too much of a good thing? If you had God in your sights any time you wanted, would you rip yourself into shreds for the salves and amusements that drag you about the collar? As the recovered say: *let go and let God.* But far too little attention is paid to how God never had a chance. If I am prevented from extolling, from *believing* by imbibing this experience whole into awe, then these clouds that stream so near to me are no more than picturesque. Then I'll be no more than stuck, a discarded wife.

I'm going with them instead. Fly me away.

Saved For Now

Thank you, every molecule of you, every color under every sky, every day: may I never slow the praise. You are the land majestic, a piece of woods wearing creek belt and prairie hat, the one. You who saw me—nearly ripped from the truce by imagining another woman standing in my place—you must have intervened.

I could let the man go but not like that, not so soon, not another woman—a client. Not while the daughters are growing, experiencing difficult puberties. Even though I ditched the camping mattress for a real bed and walk until dusk into the arms of Urban Eros.

I almost lost my mind. Some portions of it teeter to the brink still. I ask why, and I know where the site of first damage is: the terror of being no one, the terror of life without Daddy Man.

Because there lurks, always, the first holder of that title and even though cremated and stored in a proud mausoleum, I must run from him still:

Daddy, to look at you is to be a plant thirsty for sunlight. My mother carries me to your bed where you struggle to wake, and she places me in sheets next to you. She's off to subdue the curly bacon and dash your goopy eggs into solid gobs. Every morning she places me so, a toddler, into your bower where you drowse in underwear, T-shirt, sheet: all is white, soft cotton, and as if the lady of the house never made a dent.

You don't stir but emanate a presence—you know I'm there. Dreams fade to thoughts of that idiot high-school principal you will need to hold your own against today, as in many a day that you try to cram American Lit into mere kids. But what a great start to the morning: the women whose worship you willingly attend. An only daughter to stroke your T-shirt and stare at your sleeping head while you try to rise to the world.

You would not touch me: you don't have to; it is adoration I dispense. I already know that every minute you're in the house, and only then, we are alive. Later, at the breakfast table my mother will coo about me and my Daddy, and you look at me with those eyes that tunnel in so deep. You call me Electra. Mommy snickers, too, and I wonder what kind of Being Bad is this? Too many eyes are on me. You're both so big. I feel a tight pain on my face. Who or what is Electra? You won't say, and I'm shrinking: sorry for something but too stumped to say anything.

We turn to you, Daddy, to know how to feel, what to do, what's sayable, where to step and where not to. When you leave, we wait in suspension (although I play and vie for my mother's distracted attention), and when you fill the doorway on return, we gather and listen to the story about Those Assholes, the ex-coaches dumb as their footballs, plying their rules to cage students and manage literary types like you. How you flummoxed them, evaded them, trumped them. I don't understand much but walk into the halo of your laughter without fear of rebuff: if it's been a day of triumph, you pick me up, the Daddy of the sheets. The look on my mother's upturned face teaches me. Stay silent, turn to the Sun, who he is. Bask and receive the infusion, for without him we stand in life's antechamber, where nothing we do or speak or feel matters until he walks in that door and limbo is animated into the light we crave.

≈

Once a circle of us little girls sat on my lush lawn. We angled our shorts and underwear aside to show genitals to each other because we wanted to know. We guessed the big people in the house would disapprove, or in the case of my parents, exchange a glance and giggle over what Elektra was up to now. But the grass and the sun saw that we were innocent, and they shielded us. We lived part-time in this bubble of freedom—yards, runnels, vacant lots at the edge of the subdivision where weeds blocked roofs and antennae—the betwixt or overlooked corners of our world. Not for secrets did we collect there, just to lift the weight of Do This Not That. The spots were so intimate, we didn't know the word or concept of "nature." It was where we moved with one mind to cut loose or simply loll, before the sun went down.

That day we studied our soft and hairless junctures because we each had these shapes between our legs that never saw light or felt the touch of anything but our own hands, guiltily so, and we needed to confer: *mine looks like yours, pretty much? Ok. Well, that's settled.* They belonged covered up for some reason, we knew that. We slid our crotch-wear back into place without another thought and set off for the Methodist churchyard where the trees burst with fruit. We devoured gleaming handfuls but never stripped a tree.

After gorging ourselves high in the leaves we'd find a spot to plunk on the ground that was closer to the road, distancing ourselves from the old, narrow church, a clapboard two-story. It was not our church, and we never saw the goers. But we ate like their trees were ours, and afterwards we rested, in our usual cross-legged circle on the grass.

One afternoon a car zoomed past with a teenager leaning from the passenger window, blond hair split by wind, leering at us as she screamed, "Don't let the great fire god get you!"

We looked at each other and froze, making no connection to the church because it wasn't our church, sitting way back there empty and worn out. We supposed that God did check in on Sundays, but who was the Fire God? Was he hiding in the parking lot behind the church, the one place we never played? We were unhappy to be yelled at by someone the size of our babysitters, who, of course, knew everything—but whatever had this one meant?

Home for dinner, I asked my parents about the Fire God. They brushed it off. It was nothing. I was getting the Heavenly Father profile in Catholic school and couldn't leave it alone: was the Fire God the devil? Were the nuns and priests keeping a secret—a being worse than Satan who they each appeared to know and despise? The babysitter-clone was so sure though that this flaming menace was real!

What about the boy driving that car, driving her: hadn't we glimpsed him with a giant grin at the wheel? He must have agreed with her about the danger. Our parents reiterated: there was no such thing as a Fire God. The teenagers were just trying to scare us.

I chose to believe what my father said with my whole heart. He alone wove the stories that made the unseen cord pulse between us. I learned in school that God was love, and it was love for man which only meant men, a man. The man at the wheel of that teen girl's out-the-window scream was her god. The neighborhood gathered gods: fathers who sheltered wives and daughters in these warm houses on snug streets. Our gods on occasion emerged to trim the unruly grass upon which we bared our pussies and ran our apple-sticky hands.

But once, and only once, we did run yelling like banshees on steroids, back and forth across the paint-peeled porch of the silent church, peering through windows at pews in deep shadow, mad with the building's pious darkness.

≈

Asa's affair must have instigated in me these early body memories of nature, cordoned as it was in the suburbs. Was it because the first Daddy Man took the axe to trust with such a violent narcissism that I reverted to the safety of more diffuse love-objects such as the land bucolic? Do I feel a twinge of guilt that I'd thrown myself so wantonly into nature as a child? Did I learn to hide passion for the natural world in exchange for the pretense of growing up?

Girls sitting in groups on lawns or singly wandering the culverts became less a fixture of my incidental wild. Most opted for frilly bedrooms with doors closed against adults. I participated in this but couldn't discard a need for green arbors and changing sky. When puberty began its daily invasion, I resisted an unspoken admonishment: *it's not right to roam anymore. You could get hurt. You possess something that bad men will grab and take.* But flat-chested and stick-thin, I didn't believe it, and I couldn't stop walking.

I realized I was the only one of my friends still wandering our safe, uniform streets. The little ones strafed their own yards, but my peers stopped striding along like me, trailing knowledge of our extended domain. Kids on trikes zoomed driveways while I walked and walked, even down alleys of backyards so I could pet the dogs, most of them hungry for touch. I walked as far as I could before an inner alarm went off: *feet hurt, where am I?*

The day something weird happened had to have been a Saturday. Too early for my parents to notice, I'd slipped out, not that in 1965 they would have cared. In neighborhoods like these the morning flung drapes wide into living rooms, although adults were all about coffee at that hour. I took a new route looking for the unexplored. Subdivision planning made adventure scarce: the streets were an orderly grid. After a period of ambulation and amnesia, I vaguely sensed unfamiliar territory by little pleasure-bursts behind my eyes. The wild place came up on my right side, cloaked but calling.

Dense scatter of untrimmed trees bowing into a lot where a house might be nestled: neighbors would surely gossip over the owners' lack of lawn. There was no driveway. Was it a park? Or a backyard so vast you could enter already lost?

No one saw me duck in.

Drawn down a sudden slope, I entered a wonderland of ungroomed shade. The rocks were red, roomy for sitting. Water collected in a shallow wash at the bottom, and everywhere, saplings. Yet the place was navigable. It cried *see me!* as if no one had for some time.

I spied all angles for a house, a fence—nothing. The jungle of it spread wider and deeper than neighboring lots. Down at its center, I couldn't see the street above. Neither a shovel, printed sign, nor piece of trash spoke of human presence. It was simply a vacancy waiting to be deflowered by backhoes and blueprints. Who was I to be crashing around here instead of calling my friends about heading downtown to make purchases from purses of patent leather?

In loud whispers I stretched the truth and named my surrounds a *canyon*, which was ludicrous in a state where no land rose or dipped for miles. Yet the word sent goosebumps to my flesh as I surveyed this tuckaway with its dusty-rose rock benches, its dips and dives that broke the rule of the level square. I stayed, dreaming big.

These days, I was starting to worry about why boys in school didn't notice me. I knew I was yet to get the bodily bumps that they gravitated to, but that didn't stop reverie about meeting with the heartthrob of the moment, here in a secluded canyon, where we would hold hands and maybe even kiss. But something else enthralled me about this place. Climbing, crouching, scouting the scene as a time-traveler fresh from Normal, the hours turned delicious because no one knew where I was.

The way that children could trespass was a key to how we understood our state of grace. Had an owner emerged I'd be a surprise, but I'd just wave a kid-grin and leave. Crawl back up to the street

and embark on my way—I was tottering on the edge of losing that
state of grace, however.

Permission was granted to smaller bodies to wander because
they didn't own anything—and that privilege for me would soon be
lost. Puberty revoked freedom—it's the antechamber where training for ownership begins. I was about to occupy the exile of adolescence and become a danger to strangers' eyes—an outlaw, not
even beloved of Nature perhaps?

This one Saturday, I luxuriated in the unkempt property because I didn't want to give up my right to take myself any place I
pleased. I wouldn't surrender my foundation—treasured spots outdoors with their overgrowth and disarray—who allowed a few moments free from the pity that was beginning to shape my stories
about myself.

I was aging out of the knack of play, but I could still pretend. I
pretended I was far, far from the new town I was still getting to
know, eight-hundred miles from my first friends of the pussy-lawn
and church-fruit, the paradise lost when my dad moved us to further his career. It worked out. I made new pals and didn't look back.
But I kept searching for something and when I found the canyon, I
fiercely pretended it was mine.

Overhead, a blistering sun burned when I finally emerged into
a long, intuitive walk home. I never could find the canyon again. I
didn't tell my peers, who'd spent their morning watching "American Bandstand" with their feet propped in fuzzy slippers. I never
mentioned that there was a place that gave itself to me just once, a
canyon thick with green and burnished disarray, where I could forget what my body was saying or pretend that magic was as simple
as breaking the rules.

As a grown woman in talk therapy, I always left out my need
to poke around the margins—a river's edge or brushy strips of trees,
any place the houses ended or were momentarily interrupted. Even

though puberty bestowed the usual obsession with human doings, I never stopped sneaking away. I didn't hide my propensity to walk and walk for fear of misinterpretation, but because I'd accepted it, it wasn't worth mention: it boded no ambition or awards to come. I was so familiar with each hideout, I calculated that the odds of being accosted as a female alone as miniscule and besides, the world was yet to grow desperately unsafe for the likes of me. I stole away for solace and pondering, to step aside from the scrutiny of eyes and the lash of words. There were catalogues of fantasies to dip into and plenty of hurt feelings to nurse. It never occurred to me to meet the spirits the way it worked out on the acres that Asa and I bought when we married—his buffer, my classroom. I can't say I used Nature as if it were my right, but from the time I was old enough to be ordered outdoors to go play, I found to my delight it was the best thing to do. I grew into the feel of places beyond walls, drawn but not conscious it soothed the struggles of people-overload.

But with the midlife quest that resulted in a late marriage and true home, what I'd always sought—to siphon off the debris of crisis and disappointment—evolved into more: relationship within a physical intimacy that never said *I'm too tired, I hate you.* Nature was a lover that shook and shone with flagrant beauty, season after season, who was never a human monster.

In the *Diagnostic and Statistical Manual* of the therapy profession, there is no disorder based on a compulsion to be outdoors. May they never hit on the idea. Hopefully, when it comes to the natural realm, something stops the voracious architects that catalogue behavioral dos and don'ts. How we do or do not, with human others, is the only harbinger of health to them—which does seem a rationale for misuse of the natural world by site developers and smokestack fanatics. But what the denizens of diagnosis can't deny is the constancy of care that tree shade or moving water wraps around some people. It speaks to the potential for the land to heal the brokenness in us all.

Shale and dirt, rampaging weeds, mute gray of cloud bank, and feral rodents of the land chaotic: fear not. You still beat the crap out of What Men (Can) Do. Men are not worthy of worship like the land, which is first and foremost an effective antipsychotic.

I needed even stronger medicine as the midlife-turning-elder marriage teetered toward divorce. Asa was unforgiven, despite the horror of his liaison now blessedly ruptured. In the aftermath, the swirl of childhood memories, the land's silence about the affair, plus the mixture of relief and disgust that lingered (*see, he really is mean, even she couldn't stand him!*) unveiled another bridge to cross. Who would I be, after he'd so easily thrown me away?

29

After sleeping on the couch for three months following Asa's affair, I commenced a relationship with a man ten years my junior. It began the day after my sixtieth birthday.

I knew that Odysseus was never to return. I was no Penelope keeping the hearth glowing with faith. Tempted by other men, she was a wife, and the story prefers her constancy. A year after my move out, I still needed to connect with my land and did so weekly, but the contact with Asa was more strained than ever.

I never planned the arrival of the cunning man. But his brief impact on my elderhood gave me a new relish for serendipity. I could get into this kind of surprise.

At age fifty, the cunning man said he was the one who felt old, but to me he was Peter Pan. I breathed relief: he was younger, not a daddy-man, not chained to an office. Instead of a business card, he handed me a rock shaped like a heart. He understood how the soul needed to escape the artifice of town and meet itself in wild places. Once he walked from his house to the lake and back, four-teen miles. Hearing that cinched my attraction.

His Lakota ancestry drew me in; his way with stone and wood was further enticing. I fancied myself a self-styled, medicine-woman-in-training looking for my other half. This imbued the sexual charge with meaning beyond the gigantic ego-rush of the whole encounter.

The cunning man mingled easily with the natural world. He chased storms, predicting where the funnel would touch the earth. He bore inclement weather on a barely insulated back porch, while tracking contests of skill on the fake green fields of televised sports. He had jars of heart-shaped rocks and was unable to resist collect-ing them. The wooden sculptures adorning his rooms were ab-stract art in which he saw faces, surfers, birds, snow scenes, and doll houses. He hit golf balls in the backyard and rested in chairs strategically placed to absorb the sun's travels throughout the day.

Ill with COPD yet hooked on cigarettes, celiac and unable to digest fresh food, he wouldn't hear of a nutritional overhaul or nic-otine patch. Still mourning the loss of his daughter and wife after a divorce—his alcohol addiction was controlled now through a once-a-week binge—he was sensitive to any monitoring of his weekly foray downtown that ended in a bar. I didn't so much ignore his suffering as choose not to take personally every rejected offer of help.

A doting mother was his oasis. When she landed in the hospi-tal with a serious infection, he could barely stand to be in my pres-ence for worry about her. Uh oh, I'd been through *that* before.

I'm willing to answer certain charges—that I chose someone the opposite of Asa just to make a point (minus the cavalier attitude toward health, a distressing similarity, minus the mother-bond that bordered on obsessive). Maybe I wanted to pay back my husband's dalliance with his former client.

But what I found when the cunning man, by mutual agree-
ment, got ever so quickly into my head and my bed, was me. He
was my twin, my Heathcliff—what every woman thinks she wants
in her deepest loneliness. I always suspected that there but for the
grace of the gods go I—into addiction, exile, imprisonment, disease.
How I ever ended up with Asa, daughters, and the land, I do not
know.

The last thing I want to do is romanticize Indigenous persons
or ignore the pressures of personal responsibility but let us be clear.
There are individuals in whom the wounds weren't dealt by familial abuse; they are cultural, and such was the case with the cunning
man.

His relatives who lived on the reservation were an embarrassment throughout the family—merely for being "Indian." The next
generation moved into town and not only fervently tried to pass
for white, but they also forbade any discussion of their native past.

"Cunning man," tags the traditional healer of European lore.
The cunning folk, healers of the common people that were visible
from Scandinavia to Italy, persisted with their arts through the
early twentieth century, using plants, spells, symbols, hands-on
healing—whatever worked. This, rather than a Native American
shaman's apprenticeship for which he did not feel worthy, fit my
lover's eclectic approach. His back porch was the therapy room,
where many came to spill their problems and listen to his advice,
look at his art, and step into the uniqueness of his personality. He
readily and wistfully acknowledged that had love, health, school,
and work been a different story, he would have become a therapist.
The potential was obvious.

Although genetically he bore more Caucasian blood than any
other, because of the family's enduring repression of their First
World ancestry, his story is red. That he chose to reject his real
power on the medicine path is his repetition-compulsion at work,
the generations' twisted shame, ancient ways scorned as something

low-class and far less than cunning. It was a numinous and tangible past he might have redeemed. That the cunning man could see he had options but chose to hide from the world was, frankly, none of my business, and I did my best to keep out of it.

Little of this tangle was revealed the initial night, scene of a first fuck beyond a faithful marriage. I was drenched with willing intention but couldn't stay in my body. The marijuana didn't help— I'd thrown caution to the winds on that count, too, after so very long without. Foreplay was scarce but that doesn't matter; when all is heat, all is forgiven. To my mortification, a lack of female hormones made entry a challenge. If you don't use it, you lose it—so clearly that night did I verify this truth about the aging vagina. He was patient.

The man had a touching sort of pride in his penis and quite frankly it had a rare beauty about it. But attachment to being a "player" is not beautiful in a fifty-year-old man, and finally he came clean—there was another woman, had been for years.

I remembered all the compliments he'd plied me with, couched in the context of his loneliness, lamenting how he never could find anyone in our town to relate to. He painted so well a picture of a recluse who matched my monastic existence. *There was no one else,* he said that first night, and took care to maintain this story. I used to wonder why it was so hard to get on his schedule when he didn't hold a job and complained he was friendless.

Too humiliated to challenge my rival, I couldn't even think of her as such. His deceit, considering Asa's recent foray, was so disheartening, it was like having a quaff of poison in front of me that looked like wine. I knew the drink would kill; I could smell the toxic fumes, and they dismantled anything I felt for him. Profoundly sorry for my transgression against the other woman, I only wanted to skedaddle as quickly as possible, letting that stand as the apology in case she knew about me. The cunning man saw he'd crossed the line, although he terribly regretted it, and I fear it fed his aching self-hatred.

How I could watch all of this with detached sadness is beyond me.

It couldn't be because my empty wedding-ring finger felt strange anymore. I'd let that hunger to be a wife and family woman subside in a park where a stream fell over rocks. My ring went into a clear curtain of shouting water apt for carrying away pieces of former identity. I spoke to and released leaf after leaf and let go. I was learning to be truly alone and hopeful.

It wasn't that I let it go because I was the cunning man's twin, whereby anger at him would be anger at me. We were not same.

I saw his need to collect and juggle sexual experiences on the sly as more distraction from his medicine path. There was no doubt how productively he could have walked in the world, but after discovery of the lie, I finally heard what he never spelled out, loud and clear: *I don't want to.*

What was it that made the experience so easy to get over, to keep valuing its gifts despite his philandering? I felt less wronged than touched by his fears. I'd stayed an observer at the same time I immersed fully during the entire seven weeks of our relationship. I never aimed to make a commitment, and I knew why. Because some part of my soul always guessed his underlying fear to meet up with his genuine self.

I heard this denial at the perimeter of my longing, our laughter and connection, and in post-coital embrace. I heard it when we glimpsed the possibilities of the medicine path together, but he changed the subject. Throughout the hunt for bio-identical hormone creams, the new attention to moisturizing my skin, an interest in sexy bras and vibrators, I knew it: *this will never last.*

For me, the cunning man was a rite of passage, a return to the richness of sexuality when it seemed that ship had sailed. It lasted long enough to restore me, and I know I'm the one who left holding the goods. That man lost badly when I pulled away, but I'm neutral about whether he learned from it.

What I learned is that no person is "mine" enough to be subject to a makeover. If I could have extended this to a saintly nonchalance about what amounted to Asa's rejection on the backs of the Four Horsemen, well now, that *would* have been Enlightenment. But as a common woman aging into increasingly hateful times, I realized I could trust my felt knowledge of what is fair and what is unconscionable when both my work and my fun are done.

30

W hat kind of flowers burn as if direct current charges their light? I saw them fresh from the ground, but not in this world. It was a dream that woke me with a jolt: I was employed by a high school, accompanying students to job sites for the experience. The labor was menial, but usually their first work setting ever, and as teenagers what could they expect? After a bit of interface and guidance, I mostly sat around.

My dream continued. One student helped with construction on a house that looked like the one I grew up in, although more inhabited and homier. There was a warm wooden deck across the front, and a backyard that was frequented and appreciated. A big back door hung loose and worn from being opened and shut by children and busy parents.

All this I noted in the dream as an outsider. My student was working with the contractor and things went well.

Scouting for a place to sit, I was drawn to the side of the house, where a driveway separated the residences. I saw a low plant growing—a shrub, with a cluster of huge, tubular flowers. This space was very much like the real-life shaded strip between my parents' house and that of their neighbors, the ones they rarely spoke to beyond a hearty *hello!* in passing. These neighbors seemed nonexistent, since their blinds were always closed over the windows that faced our house.

Once I saw the plant in the dream, property rights ceased to matter, as did the student. The flowers glowed. There were several spikes, about a dozen, although the closer I got the more numerous they seemed. Each flower was eight to nine inches long and tumescent, on stems that burst from a clump, leaves unremarkable and ragged below. Luminosity akin to an incandescent bulb, light without the adornment of color.

Light with the substance of flesh that was without color but bright.

I struggled to classify them. Looking closely, these words came to me: *white hyacinths.* I was disappointed because it was the best I could do. They weren't hyacinths and they weren't white, I told myself in the dream. I felt I was about to fail at something, and I didn't know what or how. The blooms glowed like someone flipped their switch; they were flowers, that much is certain, but they were also that which cannot be named, cylinders of a beam that the Earth sent into this unlikely spot where no one saw but me. Their value was inestimable.

How badly I wanted to take one! Inside the dream I bargained: I want three but would settle for two. I could already see them in a vase on my mantle. I knew I wasn't at liberty to pick them; I just work here. I argued with myself: *how could anyone miss a couple from the whole clump? Should I do this? I'm on the job and could be discovered. Yet how can residents of the houses that sandwich the wonder of these lights begin to appreciate them?*

I didn't even touch them. I knew my greed outstripped rationality; out of control with wanting, I woke up. For weeks, what I called White Hyacinths—code name for Boner Plants? Penises of the Earth? The Masculine Spirit?—stayed with me. I had seen something divine and couldn't pilfer even one for lack of a rule that applied.

You can't possess the sacred, no matter how it shimmers or calls out to join you. Put it on a mantle? Hoarding a bit of the god for the sake of display—I must have known this in my dream—would dim its light and shrivel the severed root.

Earth My Body

Vagina, always dark inside, that is your nature. Wet canal in seasons of arousal or host to crone-lubes concocted to help you remember. May you wrap pleasure.

Lips of labia: flower petals. Swelled or soft unassuming, may you be kissed by a skinny-dip creek or emerge from the bush to be shown to a sunbeam.

Shy clitoris, once you get going there is no stopping you. Tiny launch-pad that rises to the scream, let the *petit mort* that is your expertise unify consciousness in space.

Molten liatris, penis stalk burning, may you find ways to cozy up to the land exotic.

Frail sac of procreative seeds, state your truth for light or firm touch, then trust it shall be given.

Less accredited—belly shoulders feet neck and the likes of up-turned palm—you are no sideline chorus here. Join your fellows in stalking the whimsy of Earth's movements.

All of you: may you meet the human hand that reaches for the sacred.

All of you: may hue and blossom craft the songs of seduction. Be played like an instrument onto ever more subtle advancements, for the mystery school—after all your roaming—is personal: the Body Vulnerable, an acolyte of soil, fire, water, and wind. Let us take apart the dogged but mistaken concept that there *are* parts discrete. We luminate the first missed lover before we can even imagine the vastness of home sweet home: flesh apostolic, emissary for the land erotic.

31

Dinner was finished, the girls had drifted off, and I was eye-ing the couch where I would sleep once again. Asa stood up, walked close to my chair and tried to hold my gaze. I clenched against the imagined barb it would take hours to extricate. But behind his look of urgency, there was more, a shyness where belligerence normally crowded in.

"Back away," I told him, expecting the worst.

Then I saw it: he wanted to comfort me. He'd put it together, the demise of the cunning man and me.

"You don't understand," he said, "I'm still in love with you."

Not like him to blurt the punchline up front. Or do an about-face on a position so cherished—"You Moved Out." I half expected a snippet of legalese to follow, a caveat that would sow a quick hedge of advantage for himself, even if it was meant as a joke. Among the load of custody battles he waded through, where parties vie to upset the applecart, the key phrase was always *a significant change in circumstance has occurred.*

"A little late, but that's nice, I guess. I'm sorry."

How knee-jerk the urge to soften the blow. I had just re-set my life, finished my niche of wife and domestic slave. I was an older gal on my own. You see them everywhere—not the frail elderly, but the chipper ones moving through errands or jobs or grandparenting without a seeming care. Glory be, I made it. Sure, something was missing. But the wonders of Urban Eros and continued ties with the land erotic in countless venues did smooth the gaps.

"Hear me out," he said, moving to perch on the edge of the couch. "Last night I sat bolt upright out of sleep. Clock said 3:00 a.m. A dream I don't remember woke me up. It was weird, but suddenly I was clear about you, me, all this separation stuff. I don't want us to be apart."

"And I'm supposed to say?"

"Stupid! I know! I've been so stupid. Not just since you moved out, either. I mean, for years. The way I always blamed shit on the stroke. I shouldn't have."

"That's nice to hear."

Again, the insipid comeback born of stun, not a bit sarcastic. This didn't come easy, not like the words among us. We were suspended in a moment where neither had the upper hand nor wanted it. Unscripted.

But *nice?* I'm not a person who hides behind *nice.* A goofy word when off-guard, it does stall the tide but what does it convey, what cascade of synonyms implied? Ducky, swell, nifty, peachy, seemly, perfectly cool? I looked at Asa with his guard decidedly down. Or did I see him at all? The power of the surprise disclosure gave birth to a sudden Nice Lady. I didn't want to hurt anybody's feelings. But I was also me-protective, that whole thing about *boundaries.* A basket of Borderline tricks could be nearby. He wasn't slamming me, and that was huge, but what did he *really* want?

A sense of the preposterous ruled, but if it was true, then it was big. It cost him a great deal to set aside the chronic anger and show a need so bare. Still, my Older Gal story seemed like the best one. You give up waiting for years to be whisked off your feet and into the arms of Prince Savior, in this case a person who cares. So here he comes, recanting and self-analyzing, and it hints at an extraordinary future. But too much too soon mars the nitty grit of Nice for a lady with a lot of baggage.

Just be nice! I used to tell the acerbic Asa. Nice not only to me and your daughters, but to the waiter you just cut to the quick and how about the salesclerk who's only chugging along your periphery? What I meant by *nice* was simply *civil*. What I meant by *nice* in reply to his big reveal, I had no idea.

Nice meant more in the confines of deep relationship. *Be nice if you cherish me.* No, that's not right either—the verb "cherish" scoots dangerously close to sentimental schlock.

Asa stood again and shifted nervously from one foot to the other like a suitor who hoped he'd be invited upstairs. He took my *too late* well but stood his ground. Now what?

I struggle to write about a man, let alone one I know as well as him. Attempts flip back to self-reference as if spring-loaded to revert. I can't enter men's heads. I am locked into my projections, my hungry ghosts asking *what can you do for me?*

In the same way, I dare not speak *for* the land. That's different from hearing it speak *to* me. We know that harmonizing with a treasured place is what small tribes do, melding the landmarks and animal-neighbors into their own histories and ways of living. A psychic merger, deep trust that Nature abides and provides, and if it doesn't, this, too, is natural law. I believe this because of relationships, so many relationships and conversations: relatives, friends, teachers, and bogeys.

But when humans only hear humans, the dictum of separateness is revered over the danger of fusion. I was steeped in the favorite admonishments of therapists past: *boundaries, boundaries!* Because one in two marriages ends in Splitsville, the smart thing is to prepare for the inevitable from day one.

A social worker once told me that deep within her agency's labyrinth where the wounded haul their secrets for healing, a co-worker defiantly placed a handcrafted placard over his lintel that read "Symbiosis is Bliss." I wonder if he'd be so defiant now. Too many decades rife with warnings about the danger of soul-merger have passed. This more than anything bodes ill for care of the land—why we can't mesh with its heart, let alone make time to know it intimately. We learn that *healthy* people are ever alert to where they begin and the other ends. The horror: what if the well-bounded ego was to falter? We also realize our sacrifice—the mystic's ecstasy exchanged for grim but predictable control inside proscribed lines.

Asa's plea for reunion came from the ether of pictures in sleep. In dreams, where are the boundaries? I had a hunch the hand of the divine might be in his dream too. I saw the white hyacinths—a visitation more than a message. Still, I said, "No thank you," and went to bed alone that night, an Older Gal open to commentary about this remarkable turn of events.

32

Austrian poet Rainer Maria Rilke stood before a museum statue of an ancient Greek god, a stone torso that spoke to him despite limbs lost to looters of yore. So overcome was he that the final lines of his poem proclaim, "There is no place here that does not see you/You must change your life." I wished for that kind of bugle call, a sign that would interpret the mandate Asa received in the wee a.m.

I didn't have to wait long for a message that slid in without fanfare as I was awake in the daylight. I think I was driving, or maybe washing the dishes or on break at work. But that's how it happens anymore. The land feeds your soul so long that nutritive truths rise to the surface when they're ready. Boink! It was not you who figured it out.

Within the worlds of psyche and soul, I am Asa. Our pain is the same. As for everyone else—yes, theirs, too. It's all one pain, the same pain.

Long before marriage-land-kids, back when I was an adult on the outside but hardly grown up inside, there was a day in therapy I was asked if I'd heard of Borderline Personality. I said no, and proceeded to listen to a vague description I mostly had to coax out of the therapist: *does it mean a space between psychotic and neurotic?* She hedged but hinted at turbulent relationships as a norm. I decided to let it out, just this once: the nature thing, how often I tromped wild places in solitary bliss or fruitful rumination.

The therapist hesitated; she was widely known for accurately pegging people to DSM criteria. Borderlines can't stand to be alone, the diagnosis-whisperer knew, and on this thorn she visibly struggled. I brushed it off, intent on ranting my whirlwind of consternation about humans I loved/hated from past and present, the agents of my torment.

I am fond of this memory and return to it often to mark the shortcomings of labels before the greatness of Nature. I used it to prove the shoe didn't fit and tossed the whole thing aside with a laugh. But like the poet in the museum who felt suddenly seen, I laughed again with a different tone when the revelation hit: she was right about me.

It all makes sense. The explosive anger that met Asa's fire with fire. The unflagging need for him, and the need to push him away. But especially how I related to emptiness and identity.

One of the reasons, despite the attraction, that I could only admire Buddhism from afar was the concept of emptiness. It scared me, deeply, like a child's fear of the dark. The void that was touted as true peace sounded like an abandoned house, a crater with no sides or bottom, the end of breath if not the fact of death. Nothingness? Buddhism holds the idea dear. But such also describes the Borderline's inner reality they're driven to flee, hence the constant drama kept churning to hold back their perceived void. Borderline reality is lack of identity, it's emptiness—uncertainty that oneself even exists, as if the body were a trick of the equally void-threatened mind.

Who squashes identity in formation? The empty-souled parent(s), of course, inheritors of worthless distaste for themselves. Asa's younger days held plenty of that trauma, and I, too, learned fearfully to step around the big people's moods. Too many times surprised by their sudden rages, their contempt, their surety when they leveled, "you're wrong!" and "how could you?" Nominally followed up with the ever petulant "but we *love* you!" As if no matter what, they deserved a reward for this.

Luckily, I stumbled onto an identity through the land—through palominos ridden on overgrazed fields and tiny canyons discovered in the burbs. Luckily, I never outgrew these havens, never accepted the script that out-of-doors is an occasional sideline to the importance of Busy, the scuttle for money and love—landscape as a treat while waiting to get back in the game as soon as possible.

I had an advantage with the land erotic. Enrolled in its courses at midlife, with graduate work during menopause: hours visiting a creek, veering off paths into woods, scanning all horizons Up Top. The lessons spilled past the brackets of property lines when I found lost parts of my suppressed soul in city parks, by a campus pond, or any wild space where I could take a vacation from the To Do List.

Over the years the love for and from these places shaped my identity, but most of the time I didn't know that; I felt empty, lost in space. I didn't craft an identity that was land-based simply by relaxing into pretty scenes. I had to listen and face sore truths. I made a review of deeds plus endured assaults by emotion, yes. But finally, I found the Great All, which was not a void, but a full and beautiful throng, a multitude, a platter of terrene delights on this big blue marble. Mine was an identity found through home, which was everywhere. Eros was the vital spark to join body and Earth.

The sorrow is immense when facing that in my culture, there is no place for the priestess who reads nature, who catalogues the secrets that are so plain for all to hear. How to share the ecstasy? How do mystics ever tell anyone anything? Through words from the pencil, pen, or keyboard. If poetry edges the lines, the caress is tender and pleasurable on their way to the surface. After suffering the "words among us" as weapons, I remake swords into plowshares of song.

Over time, I learned to take in the night, from the front deck that sat like a prow on our family's house, with the dark, heavy, and plush sky—a teeming, populated, conversant void held under so many stars. I was never alone, even without my body, which seemed to flutter under the sky—in this way the Borderline's "dissociation" was not my reality. The drama of seasons, weather, sun, and moon became far more enticing than my scenarios with people. Is this madness? Or a turn of heart so simple everybody used to go there?

Tat tuam asi or translated from the Sanskrit: *Thou art that.* Who isn't that? No one.

I realized I'd settled into a view of me and the land versus Asa, then labeled him the first cause in our battles and separation. How else to explain the enduring ache that was a marriage careening from crisis to calamity?

But witness the aging Borderline: less manifest chaos, fewer rage fits, emptiness looming only a little. Many release the dull residue of despair into recovery. I took the first step when I moved to the land. I stopped collecting new people, tussling with them psychologically then running away, and became solitary. Asa quit his weekend-drunk role when the kids came along. The words among us contained our acting-out inside the house that devolved into Borderline antics when pushed.

Asa did assuage himself with food, unhealthy food and lots of it. He was diabetic and in denial; he worked like work was the teat from which all self-respect streamed. My addiction was to him—worrying, managing, waiting for the next gunshot of character assassination, the next dramatic pull away from intimacy. I was the Borderline Patrol and with my mission—to say I am not that, but *he is*. After a cardio-cerebral catastrophe at the center of our lives, I couldn't bear the possibility that stroke invades character like an occupying army that never leaves. Nor could I release Daddy Man from his assigned post. Escaping into Urban Eros, I quit my role with Asa as stand-in for Mom, the victim wife.

Kind of.

Get lost, but I'll come over when I want to.

But if *I am that* what *is* that, and how is it we *all are that?*

Being part narcissist, Borderlines must be serviced, saved, praised, and given that lifeline of attention at all costs—though clearly a person so desperate to be seen was once a child consistently erased. This is but one way abused children react, filling the ranks of the BPD-diagnosed. But who is not abused by the pressure placed on unnaturally nuclear families that break under the strain all too often? Women still are considered the Eve and grief of humanity. How isn't the epidemic of frantic jostling for celebrity a serious cry for help?

Digging deeper into the elaborated picture of BPD, one finds amazing parallels to a daughter whose struggles I know too well. The sensory overload that characterizes the Borderline parallels the frightening overwhelm a person with autism can feel. Like the scads of Lyme sufferers who are told their disability is all their heads, we can add BPD to this club of the disbelieved. "Autism is just better reporting, Lyme sufferers are hypochondriacs, BPD is really depression or addiction." Each is a neurological strain, an under-funded research opportunity, and an existential crisis. But what has the land to do with any of it?

The underdogs claim autism is caused by environmental toxins: vaccines, antidepressant use in the womb, pesticides, or

Pitocin. BPD is purported only to be caused by poor human relationships. But aren't we all laced with froth from the industrial age?
We tacitly accept cancer as the consumer's price to pay for a bevy
of mass-made neurotoxic goods, while further consequences pile
up. Emotional lability is a common thread.

How can this be? Because pollutants don't just get on our
nerves; they strip them. They inflame them. They stunt them,
shortening the dendrites, those branches reaching out from nerve
cells to pass vital information along.

If I feel like a stripped wire walking, I don't want you near—
I'm too tender, it hurts. But wait, don't go away, I have human
needs and I'm terrified of the void. Hence the Borderline's con-
founding refrain: *don't leave me, get out of here!*

I go to my land and pretend its touch is pure while chemicals
mist from the many-spigoted Ag-monsters rolling the fields
nearby. I claim virtue because at least I protect one parcel from a
modicum of assault. But I know that when it rains, not all that falls
is water. Maybe the giant sycamore or the fawn I stopped for in the
road would also bitch like a raw-nerve Borderline if they could.

I am that. One pain, the same pain. Whether first cause is the
xenobiotic flood of substances new to the fabric of daily living, or
whether we got off track because all roads from Greed lead here,
we are creatures in the same boat, traveling the borderline between
paranoia and a faint memory of safety and symbiosis.

The Earth's mood swings of late seem ominous. It's so easy to
call catastrophic weather the revenge of Mother Nature. But when
fish are born eyeless with oozing lesions, where is the emotional
pain located? In their flesh? In the water? In the souls of you and
me?

≈

I found it ludicrous to call the meno- and andro- thing a
"pause" once I could look backwards at both. Better termed Uproar,
Reckoning, Change—but into what? Such a sweeping loss of the

known can create a desert or rain down blooms. For Asa, it was a door to further decline of his body and mind. I have survivor's guilt.

But if something is to be redeemed it is this: which one of us loved the land with physical presence and conscious erotic devotion? The land: I didn't go to it with a prescription or health agenda. I ran there when I hurt because I couldn't remember a time when it didn't call me to come.

Say I never stopped being that girl in a dark churchyard gobbling fresh fruit from laden trees. The first shattering body-uproar—puberty—sent me looking for people-devoid wild spaces when my peers forsook them, because I craved safety and peace. When menopause stripped hormones and rearranged perspective in a years-long assault, it was clear the land was in on what I felt. Not only because it was no stranger to aging and decay. It's the relationship angle I wish to emphasize, and there's plenty to go around.

Elders often develop a lust for gardening. It looks and sounds amorous, because suddenly they care less about what the Joneses will think of their yard and more for the moment: hands digging deep in the dirt or lingering over the beauty that wakes in their plot. We call them garden *beds*. This is a fractal of the land erotic's message. May they expand that lived thrill into encounters with every tree or creek*bed* that tries to get their attention. And by the Earth may they feel loved.

Not always does a bed imply sex, but it does invite a disconnect from the chatter within and without, another realm of which even sleep is most mysterious.

You want to be alone—you pausing woman or man, you elder feeling empty and afraid—yet you don't. You can't get it up or let it in, but the land doesn't care. It holds the salve, it is the hospital, and it has some homework for you. It says *give me your tired genitals, your paper skin, your crate-loads of regret. I am the land in constant flux, dying and rebirthing wet then dry then back to slathering. I am the home where you have always fit in, never more giving than now when you're reminded that you, humans—though not me, until the oceans boil, or the red giant comes roasting—will see an end to your flesh and your attachment to here.*

33

Both daughters were spending the night elsewhere. A storm built slowly after dusk, shouting proximity with bright flashes devoid of thunder. Simply strobes: arcs on the horizon, whiteouts in the yard.

Asa and I lay with our feet to that fire. Our bed pointed to a window where we could see the light-show advance. We were naked and well past our prime. I mentioned that people have been struck by lightning inside their rooms. "I know," he said.

But we continued to hold hands, side-by-side. A candle burned as talisman: sympathetic magic. A little flame inside, so that lightning may harbor its bolts to the sky.

A little flame inside. Little place, enormous impact. With fingers that learned over two decades where to probe, Asa was the man I remembered. My sex was puffy with absorbed estrogen, courtesy of cohosh and wild yam, and the clitoral hood peeked tentatively. A current ran with his touch, flared with the lightning strikes that seemed to highlight the clothesline out back. A start, a flush, a target touched, then a subsiding. We build momentum for our lovers the way the rhythm of the nervous system goads a body onward: sprint, rest, renew the push.

Then a second rhythm wanted in. Each time a flash of light braised the window, I surged with excitement, regardless of a hand on me. In the rest-moment as Asa held back, there it was: a strike against the pane, and I nearly came. Transferred excitement? Mixed up neurons firing at random stimuli? Was this some storm god toying with an open channel, charged electrical particles endowed with intention? Who guides this ascent to jagged pleasure—a finger of flesh or a finger of light?

At last, the land and I were one.

Science tells how it's done. "Streamers" from the ground form a pathway up to the restless cloud, inviting the spark. The heat builds up on the way down.

The heat builds up on the way down. But when I finally dissolved, unsure if it was Asa's doing or 50,000 amps of energy compressed into tentacles of light, the place was not "down." It was center, the center of a splaying wheel of arms and legs, a united hub. At the center of motion, stillness gathered up for more. At the center of my body, a detonation, the shattering of mind into vocals that peppered the room.

What if we are streamers, step ladders reaching to ditch the self's prattle about yesterday and tomorrow? Who can entirely forget our waltz with the non-rational, nonverbal world? Is it so fearful to think *homo loquens* may not be superior? On this night, I took off my smarty-pants and gave up to the firebolt. If lightning can fling a human into orgasm, there is hope we may fall helplessly, romantically, in love with the ripply, spiky, scent-swept, color-whomped levin-needled land—forever home again.

Epilogue

In 2017, Asa suffered his fifth stroke, spent a week in the hospital, then made his way to the spirit world. Three years prior, he'd had a doozie that rendered him incapable of working as an attorney, or of working at all. That second stroke was a massive brain bleed that rendered substantial portions of his vision occluded, which affected his balance, although speech centers remained untouched. He couldn't track complex thoughts, and without clients to focus on, he had no social life. He knew he was finished as a working man, and he could no longer drive or walk on uneven surfaces or read a book, and he became deeply depressed.

I moved back into the house and became his caregiver. Our daughters were still in high school. Sierra graduated and Nina moved to a group home before his death from stroke number five. Strokes three and four were extremely stressful events for our family, but minor medical events that resulted in him being released from the hospital the day after.

We moved into town because we could no longer afford the farm that wasn't. The bank foreclosed on the property, and eventually deer hunters bought it. They tore down our house, erected two-story blinds to spy on their prey, and planted corn to attract them.

Asa's death was, for me, an experience of walking up to the entrance of the otherworld and peering into the mist as he crossed. There were many strange synchronicities that left me with much to ponder about an afterlife as I lived in suspension, self-identified as a widow for years. Land that I now could only access on public grounds was my grief counselor and confidante. With its help, I concluded that Asa was the love of my life, and there would be no other, even as I eventually explored online dating.

Our daughters are now in their mid-twenties and reaching for their own independent lives, although Nina will always need twenty-four-hour support. I see her frequently throughout the week and still manage her medical situation but am grateful that she is in a residential setting and day center where she is cherished and protected, truly seen for her ability to touch hearts without guile or manipulation.

One winter solstice, I met a twin soul my age, a man who lost his wife of decades to an ugly divorce and entered the darkness that grief wraps around us when the void is cut from too severe a cloth. Together, we have found that the elder years are best suited to truth and kindness, and we endeavor to live that in relationship to each other. We are best friends and lovers who have come to share a cabin in the woods where we reflect on our lives, share the insights, and try to bring forth a mindful "retirement," freed from the usual worries and distractions.

In short, I feel blessed. Ravaged by past losses heavy as baggage that needs shipping off to the ether, yes. How can there *still* be so much to process after so many years? But I returned to a gorgeous seclusion among towering oaks only ten miles from the original land erotic. It dawns on me that there is no logical nor spiritual sense in stuffing my identity into the file cabinets of grief anymore. Health allows me to investigate the trails and lakeside that are my new home. I experience resurrection by the resplendence of the Earth opening me to *now*-loving delight.

May each human striving on this alluring planet find hope. May we return to the idea of the evolution of consciousness: beyond war, past divisions based on race or political bent. May flesh know and truthful brain gather the healing touch of flower and stalk, water on the move, comfy rock ledges and blue winter skies lit stark upon the retina. May Her overheated body heaving with weather that threatens survival be lulled into balance by our ardor. May the land—whether Arctic, temperate, or tropic—be your supreme lover for life.

About the Author

Sue Westwind is also the author of *Lunacy Lost: A Memoir of Green Mental Health*. She has been a holistic mental-health coach and holds a bachelor's degree in education and a master's degree in religious studies from the University of Kansas. She developed workshops on the topics of earth-based spirituality and natural mental health and taught a course called "Natural Mind" with integrative practitioners, and "Mind in Nature" as an ecotherapist. To learn more about Sue Westwind, please visit her website at suewestwind.com, where she regularly blogs. She can be reached via email at sue@suewestwind.com, and she welcomes correspondence from readers.

Lightning Source UK Ltd.
Milton Keynes UK
UKHW020800031022
409835UK00011B/1224

9 780996 559287